The Coaches' Strength and Conditioning Training Toolkit

John Cissik

ISBN: 978-1-60679-317-6
Library of Congress Control Number: 2014948875
Book layout: Cheery Sugabo
Cover design: Cheery Sugabo
Front cover photos: iStock/Thinkstock
Text photos: Chuck Shanlever
Illustrations: Vyacheslav Biryukov/iStock/Thinkstock (Chapter 4); vizualbyte/iStock/
          Thinkstock (Chapter 9)

Coaches Choice
P.O. Box 1828
Monterey, CA 93942
www.coacheschoice.com

Acknowledgments

A number of people help to make a book like this possible. I would like to thank my wife Ewa and my kids Hektor, Marcus, and Duncan for the patience and support during this process. Kristi Huelsing and Jim Peterson from Coaches Choice were a pleasure to work with again, always communicating clearly what the expectations are, and making this process as painless as possible.

I would also really like to thank the models in this book. Taking photos of exercise technique is an interesting experience. No matter how much weight is being used, holding these positions while the camera adjusts can be a challenging experience for even the fittest person. Even with modern digital photography, this can still be a lengthy process, especially with the 150 photos that are in this book. Jordan Karnes and Tinesha Bustos were all very patient during this process, and their help was invaluable.

Finally, I would like to thank Texas Woman's University for the use of their Fitness and Recreation Center during the shooting of the photographs in this book.

Contents

- Change the Body
- Improve Performance
- Prevent or Rehabilitate Injuries

- Train for Goals
- The Only Easy Day Was Yesterday
- Pay Dues

- Warming Up
- Understanding When an Athlete Is Hurt
- Staying Safe

- Squats
- Hip Extension Exercises
- Presses
- Rows/Pulls
- Power Cleans
- Power Snatches
- Jerks

- Swings
- Cleans
- Snatches
- Jerks
- Get-Ups
- Windmills
- Farmer's Walk

- Develop the Structure
- Determine the Broad Goals and Tools for Each Period of Training
- Plan the Details Four Weeks at a Time

- Short-Term Objectives
- Long-Term Objectives

Introduction

Strength and conditioning has been an emerging field over the last 30 years. Over this time period, it has been regarded as indispensable for the preparation of athletes. Strength and conditioning improves performance, prevents injuries, and is used to help rehabilitate injuries.

The coaching of strength and conditioning is part science and part art. The science has established a foundation concerning how exercise works and what it does. However, the science has not yet effectively established the most optimal ways of applying strength and conditioning. This is where the art of coaching comes in. The coach must try new things, assess their effectiveness, and remain flexible in the conditioning of their athletes.

Over the last 30 years, the field of strength and conditioning has changed radically, and the expectations placed upon its coaches have also changed. Thirty years ago, strength and conditioning meant a weight room dominated activity primarily focused around the Olympic lifts and the bench press, squat, and deadlift. Today, that is still a part of strength and conditioning; indeed, it still makes up the foundation of the weight room work. However, today a strength coach is expected to understand the use of other implements such as kettlebells, heavy ropes, suspension training, and sandbags. In addition, there is an expectation to apply strength and conditioning to the sport via speed training, agility training, and plyometrics. In other words, the toolkit for a strength and conditioning coach has expanded greatly over the last 30 years.

Accompanying the expansion in the tools that a strength and conditioning coach can use is a great degree of marketing about each tool. This is not surprising; marketing alerts the coach to the existence of the tool and seeks to convince a coach that a tool is needed. This is usually by attempting to make a new tool seem to be the "best" strength and conditioning tool and to establish that it is better than the others. As very little research is available on the newer strength and conditioning tools, this is largely done via testimonials. For example, Athlete X uses this tool or Coach Y advocates its use. With the expansion in social media over the last few years, marketing has become even easier.

The challenge to any coach is to filter through all this information. No matter the level at which an athlete competes, athletes have a very limited amount of time to train. Athletes also have a limited ability to recover from training. These two facts are further complicated by the fact that strength and conditioning has to complement and support the athlete's sports training. This means that any training tool that is selected, any exercise that is included in an athlete's program, has to make the best possible use of the athlete's limited time and recovery ability. This is a challenge given the noise surrounding most of the training tools and their approaches.

It is the intent of this book to introduce the coach to the various training tools that are employed today. This will include "traditional" exercises like the squat and the power clean as well as newer exercises like sandbags. After introducing the tools, this book will provide a framework to help the coach make decisions about which tools to employ and how to use them.

This book is organized into three parts. The first part provides the background to strength and conditioning—why it's used, what it does, how to use it effectively, and how to employ it safely. The second part provides an overview to the various training tools (free weights, kettlebells, suspension trainers, heavy ropes, sandbags, and speed/agility/plyometric exercises). Exercises are described and extensively illustrated. The final part covers how to incorporate these tools into an effective training program.

This book is primarily geared toward the sports coach and to the athlete that is a consumer of strength and conditioning. Hopefully, this book provides some perspective and helps the reader wade through the marketing, hype, and testimonials. Many of the tools described in this book are extremely effective, but there is no best. There is only best for specific situations, and understanding that will help to maximize the athlete's training time.

PART I Background

Part I of this book is meant to provide the background behind the strength and conditioning of athletes. It provides an overview of the hows and whys behind using strength and conditioning. It's divided into three chapters: the first deals with why people train, the second deals with principles of training, and the third deals with safety.

The first chapter describes the benefits that athletes receive from training. Understanding these benefits is important for the coach. These benefits are the motivation behind incorporating strength and conditioning into a program. Benefits may include changing the athlete's body, improving performance, or preventing or rehabilitating injuries.

The second chapter provides the foundational principles that underlie successful strength and conditioning programs. These principles make strength and conditioning a deliberate, focused, and successful process that addresses an athlete's needs. Failing to apply these principles means that any performance improvement is by chance and may not use the athlete's limited time well.

The third chapter is important for keeping training a safe and effective process. Clearly, athletes should not be injured while performing strength and conditioning. This chapter discusses how to warm up to prevent injuries, how to understand the difference between being sore and being hurt, and how to stay safe in the strength and conditioning environment.

Chapter 1 Why People Train

Athletic strength and conditioning has become extremely popular in the last 10 years. It is a fun and effective way to improve fitness. This chapter is going to describe why people train and the benefits they achieve as a result of training. Essentially, people train for the following reasons:
- Change the body
- Improve performance
- Prevent or rehabilitate injuries

Change the Body

One of the biggest reasons why people train is to change some aspect of the body. Normally, this refers to how they look. Combined with sensible nutrition, training is an extremely effective way to increase the size of the muscles, how the muscle fibers are oriented, and the make-up of the muscles.

Muscles are made up of muscle fibers. These are the cells of the muscle. Each muscle fiber runs the entire length of the muscle. The size of the muscles is increased through a process called hypertrophy, which means that the muscles grow as a result of each muscle fiber becoming larger. Some of this process is influenced by training, some by nutrition, and some of it is limited by genetics.

With regard to training, it must be kept in mind that larger muscles are more metabolically expensive than smaller muscles. This means they require more energy to maintain than smaller muscles. As a result, it is difficult to "persuade" the body to increase the size of the muscles. This must be done from training that is difficult enough and repeated enough that there is no other option than to increase the size of the muscles in order to accommodate the demands of the training.

Nutrition is important because it fuels workouts, so that an athlete can train at the intensity necessary to increase muscle mass. It is important because it provides the ingredients for making the muscle fibers larger. It is also important because proper nutrition helps to ensure that an athlete isn't gaining a lot of fat while attempting to increase muscle size.

Genetics has a role in muscle size. Hormone levels and hormone response to exercise are influenced by genetics. The hormones help to tell the body what to do as a result of training. In addition, within the membrane that surrounds each muscle fiber are cells called satellite cells. These are extremely important to muscle fiber hypertrophy, though their exact role isn't completely understood today. People with fewer of these cells are very limited in their ability to experience hypertrophy, whereas someone with many of these cells responds very favorably to this type of training.

Not only can muscle fibers grow as a result of training, they can change their orientation within the muscle. Muscle fibers don't only run straight up and down; they may run at an angle to the tendon. As a result of training, this angle can increase, which allows for increased strength and muscle hypertrophy. This process is done by focusing on training that increases strength and muscle fiber hypertrophy. The orientation can also decrease, which allows for them to shorten more quickly. This process is done through power and speed training.

The orientation of the muscle fibers is an important adaptation as there is a trade-off from training. As these muscle fiber angles increase, they tend to shorten more slowly. This result won't be important to most people, but to individuals concerned about their sprinting speed, this could prove to be a problem. This is one reason why the training of many track athletes does not focus on hypertrophy training very heavily.

A range of muscle fiber types is found in the human body. These fiber types range from one extreme, called slow-twitch muscle fibers, to the other extreme, called fast-twitch muscle fibers, with many types in between. Slow-twitch muscle fibers provide a very small amount of force, but are extremely difficult to fatigue. Good distance runners, cyclists, swimmers, or other type of endurance athletes are going to want to have a lot of slow-twitch muscle fibers. Fast-twitch muscle fibers provide a great amount of force, are larger, but fatigue very quickly. In order to be good at lifting heavy weights, sprinting, jumping, or throwing, an athlete is going to need a lot of fast-twitch muscle fibers.

The bad news is that everyone is born with a certain percentage of each. It does not appear that percentage of fast-twitch muscle fibers in the body can be increased. This represents another genetic limitation to performance on speed, strength, and power activities. However, the percentage of slow-twitch muscle fibers can be increased at the expense of the fast-twitch ones. This process can be done as a result of too much endurance-type training. This should help to reinforce the need to focus training around an athlete's goals.

Improve Performance

Strength and conditioning improves athletic performance. It does so by improving physical abilities that impact an athlete's ability to perform. These abilities include strength, power, speed, agility, and endurance.

Strength

Strength is the ability to exert force. A lot of things come together to help make someone stronger as a result of training. These factors include developing the muscles, better skill at performing the exercises, and better control by the brain and spinal cord.

In terms of developing the muscles to enhance strength, a number of elements need to be considered. First, larger muscles have the potential to be stronger ones. This means that training that is geared toward hypertrophy can provide the foundation for future strength gains. Second, training for hypertrophy also helps to reorient the angles of the muscle fibers, improving their potential to generate force. Finally, training that focuses on developing the fast-twitch muscle fibers also will lead to an increase in strength. All of this means that it is important to precede maximal strength training with hypertrophy-oriented training to help provide the foundation.

Even the simplest exercises require a lot of technique. Solid technique on the exercises puts an athlete into position to be able to lift more weight; poor technique makes the exercise more difficult to perform. This takes time to learn and must continually be refined as athletes progress through their training lifetime.

Strength is also a skill that the body, particularly the nervous system that controls the muscles, must learn through practice. The brain has to learn how to recruit the greatest number of muscle fibers in the shortest amount of time to perform the exercise. The brain and spinal cord need to learn how to quiet the opposing muscle groups that interfere with an untrained individual's ability to execute exercises. The muscles, tendons, ligaments, and nervous system also have a number of protective mechanisms that are extremely conservative when it comes to lifting heavy weights, and these systems are reset as a result of training.

Power

Power is the ability to express strength quickly. A number of factors are essential to increasing power as a result of training. These factors include developing the muscles, strength, skill, and better control by the brain and spinal cord.

When it comes to developing the muscles to enhance power, the development of the fast-twitch muscle fibers is essential. Remember, not only are they larger, and not only do they generate more force, but they also generate force more quickly than the slow-twitch muscle fibers. This means that when power is the goal, training programs have to be organized in such a way that they focus on fast-twitch muscle fibers and minimize training that emphasizes the slow-twitch muscle fibers.

Strength is essential to power and is a limiting factor. Not only does strength limit power, but strength is important to reaping the full benefits from many of the exercises that focus on power, like plyometrics. Individuals that are stronger get more benefits from power training than individuals that are not as strong. This means that a foundation of strength must be at least maintained if not increased when athletes are striving to increase their power.

As with strength, exercises that improve power require a great deal of skill. Unlike strength exercises, which tend to be performed slowly, exercises that improve power are performed extremely quickly. This does not leave a lot of time to correct errors during the exercise, so mastering these movements takes time.

Finally, when it comes to power, the brain and spinal cord must balance several elements in a short period of time. They must learn to recruit a large number of muscle fibers, to generate a large amount of force, and they must quiet some of those protective reflexes. All of this has to happen in a very short period of time. This process takes time to learn and perfect.

Speed

Speed is how fast an individual moves. In general, speed is dependent upon several factors. These factors include strength, the ability of the brain and spinal cord to recruit muscle fibers, the make-up of the muscles, and the development of the components of speed.

Strength is important because running involves exerting force against the ground. To a point, being able to exert more force against the ground means being able to be potentially faster. As with power and strength, speed is also dependent upon the ability of the brain and spinal cord to recruit a number of muscle fibers quickly. It is also highly dependent on the make-up of the muscles (i.e., the fast-twitch muscle fibers).

Speed has three components: acceleration (increasing speed), maximum velocity (the greatest speed that can be reached), and speed endurance (the ability to maintain speed and resist fatigue). Each of these components has running techniques that are slightly different, and each has its own unique approaches to training. This process will be detailed more in Chapter 9.

Note that speed is situation-dependent. So it could refer to the speed with which a barbell moves, swimming speed, cycling speed, or such. Regardless of the situation, speed is trained with maximum efforts, focusing on good technique, with complete recovery between efforts.

Agility

Agility is the ability to change directions. It involves the summation of many abilities: the ability to see and react to a stimulus, the ability to exert force against the ground, being able to maintain balance, decelerate, and accelerate, and so forth. It is extremely challenging to train because it is situation-specific, which makes it difficult to train for as it is impossible to anticipate and duplicate in a training program every possible situation that an athlete might encounter.

Due to that challenge, agility is typically trained by addressing a number of physical qualities while teaching foundational movements than can hopefully carry over to various situations. The qualities that are important for agility include mobility, strength, power, and speed while fundamental movement patterns (see Chapter 9) are addressed. Agility is believed to be limited by mobility, strength, power, speed, as well as the make-up of the muscles, and the ability of the brain/spinal cord to recruit large numbers of muscle fibers quickly.

Endurance

Endurance is the ability to exert force over time. This quality is highly situation-specific, and different individuals have different needs. For example, someone interested in running a marathon has different endurance needs than someone training for strongman competitions. Endurance training is primarily geared toward building up energy stores within the muscles, developing muscle fibers, as well as developing volitional qualities.

In terms of energy storage, endurance training increases the ability to do work for longer periods of time. This process is accomplished by increasing the amount of energy stores located in the muscles. It is also achieved via two other methods. One method involves increasing the quantities of the enzymes that limit the rate and amount of energy stores that the body breaks down for fuel. The other method involves selectively sparing some fuel sources (for example, glycogen) in favor of others (fat) with greater fitness levels.

Endurance training, like strength and power training, selectively enhances certain types of muscle fibers, which is dependent upon the type of training done. Training that focuses on long durations (for example, jogging) enhances slow-twitch muscle fibers. Training that focuses on shorter durations and higher intensity enhances different types of fast-twitch muscle fibers. Developing these muscle fibers improves endurance performance.

Finally, it should be pointed out that endurance training develops the ability to tolerate levels of fatigue. Many times, the brain will quit before the body does. Training geared toward improving endurance helps to push back those mental barriers to fatigue.

Prevent or Rehabilitate Injuries

In addition to enhancing muscular development and improving performance, training can also be used to prevent injuries or to rehabilitate injuries after they occur. Injuries may be due to contact, faulty movement patterns, muscle imbalances, lack of fitness, and poor flexibility. While training cannot do much to prevent contact injuries, it can address many of the other causes of injury.

Strength and conditioning prevents and rehabilitates injuries in several ways. First, it allows an athlete to strengthen all of the muscles around a joint, which prevents muscular imbalances from occurring. Second, it strengthens soft tissue like ligaments and tendons that are often the weak links during performance. Third, it helps to enhance other fitness qualities that may be weak links, such as mobility or endurance. Finally, these exercises help to teach and reinforce good movement patterns in activities such as sprinting, jumping, and changing directions.

Chapter 2 Principles of Training

Chapter 1 covered the adaptations that the body makes as a result of training. It is important to understand that these adaptations are not accidental or a result of chance; rather, they are something that can be very deliberately planned and worked for. Training isn't supposed to be something that is random. If it is random, then improvements are left to chance. In other words, athletes might make gains, they might waste their time, they might get injured; anything is possible. To keep this from happening, several principles can serve as the foundation for training:

- Train for goals.
- The only easy day was yesterday.
- Pay dues.

Train for Goals

The gains that are made from training are not a result of accident; they are a result of a careful, methodical approach designed to get an individual where they want to go. Everyone wants to get somewhere from their training. Some want to be better at a specific sport, some want to be stronger, faster, more muscular, smaller, and so forth. It is important to think this process through and then put together a training program designed to accomplish an athlete's goals. Failing to do so can result in a waste of time and energy as training is spent working on something that an athlete is not interested in. For example, if a goal is to improve an athlete's time in running the 5 km race, spending a lot of time in the gym improving bench press won't help racing time. This section will describe how to train for different goals.

The idea of training for goals applies to the muscles that are used, specific movement patterns, rest, and the speed at which that training is performed. Whenever possible and practical, training should be organized to address these four factors (muscles, movements, rest, and speed) in a manner similar to what an athlete is training for. Two examples will follow.

The first example deals with improving 5 km running performance. The 5 km race is a popular distance and is run in the 12- to 30-minute range. It is an activity primarily using the lower body, though the trunk and core muscles are important for good technique, and the arm swing is important for balance and speed. It is a continuous movement, so anyone running the 5 km race will be running nonstop the entire time.

People that run races of this sort typically experience a range of potential injuries, including hamstring strains, quadriceps/patellar tendon injuries, stress fractures to the legs, and shin splints.

A program designed to train the 5 km runner should address several areas. First, the runner needs the endurance to be able to run the entire distance. Second, the runner needs to be able to cover the distance quickly. Third, the runner needs to be able to run the race and conduct the training safely.

To improve the ability to run the entire distance, the distance that the runner covers in endurance training sessions is gradually increased. This approach will vary depending upon where the runner is starting. The distance should not be increased by more than 10 percent per week because the body needs a chance to become adjusted to the increased demands. Increasing distance too quickly is a leading cause of shin splints and stress fractures. For example, one day a week might be devoted to endurance running. The workouts might look like the following:

- Week 1: 2 miles
- Week 2: 2.2 miles
- Week 3: 2.5 miles
- Week 4: 2.75 miles
- Week 5: 3 miles
- Week 6: 3.3 miles

To improve the ability to improve speed, a number of training tools can be employed. First, it's important to practice running quickly, which is done by covering smaller distances with great speed. Since this is a distance event, and not a short sprint, this practice is done in a manner that does not allow for much rest in between each sprint. In addition, this process should be approached gradually, as this very intense training method can increase the risk of injury. Second, other training tools like heavy ropes, kettlebells, and suspension training can be used to help the runner endure running at speed. Finally, increasing strength will help to increase speed. A sample training program to address this approach is outlined in Figure 2-1.

The workouts described also address the safety aspect in several ways. First, distances are gradually increased, which addresses all of the injury concerns. Second, the hamstrings are addressed via both strength training and warming up before the workouts. Third, the tendon issues are addressed via strength training and the conditioning workout. Finally, the shin splint/stress fracture concerns are addressed via warming up, strength training, and the conditioning workout.

Often, individuals forget to train those muscles that they cannot see in the mirror. This sets athletes up for imbalances at joints and possible injuries. The muscles of the upper back are a great example. Most males like to train their chest, shoulders, and triceps, but may not focus adequately on the muscles of their upper back. The pull-up

Day 1	Day 2	Day 3	Day 4	Day 5
Endurance run: 2 miles	Strength training: • Back squats, 3x10–15x60–70% • Leg press, 3x10–15 • Romanian deadlift, 3x10–15 • Calves, 3x15–20	Conditioning (Perform each exercise for 30 seconds, rest 60 seconds after all the exercises have been performed, repeat three times.): • Kettlebell swings • Heavy rope slams • Suspension rows • One-arm kettlebell swings • One-arm rope slams • Suspension push-ups • Kettlebell snatch • Heavy rope wood choppers • Suspension reverse flies • Heavy rope circles • Kettlebell clean • Suspension knees to chest	Interval running: • 300-meter sprints, 5x, walk for 90 seconds between each sprint	Strength training: • Dumbbell bench press, 3x10–15 • Pull-ups, 3x10–15 • Dumbbell shoulder press, 3x10–15 • Biceps/triceps, 3x10–15 each

Figure 2-1. Sample workout program to help with running fast

is one of the best all-around exercises for the muscles of the upper back, and is one of those exercises that individuals are generally not very good at.

The pull-up is a very specific movement pattern involving the muscles of the upper back and biceps lifting the body up so that the chin clears the pull-up bar. It requires enough strength to pull the body up; after that, it takes a combination of strength and endurance to perform this exercise. Once athletes can perform 10 to 12 repetitions, they can even consider performing pull-ups with additional weight.

The pull-up is best mastered by performing that exercise along with exercises that target the muscles of the upper back and biceps. For people that cannot perform very many pull-ups, the eccentric pull-up (jump up, take as long as possible to lower oneself down) is the place to start. This modified pull-up is then supplemented with the other exercises. Eventually, athletes can perform as many pull-ups as possible prior to the eccentric pull-ups, followed by the other exercises. Figure 2-2 shows what such workouts might look like, comparing week 1 and week 16 to show how a person could progress.

	Week 1	Week 16
Maximum Number of Pull-Ups Possible	0	4
Sample Workout	Eccentric pull-ups, 5x Pulldowns (with pull-up grip), 3x8–12 Bent-over rows, 3x8–12 Biceps curls, 3x8–12 Wrist curls, 3x8–12	Pull-ups, 5xMax Eccentric pull-ups, 3x Pulldowns (with pull-up grip), 3x8–12 Bent-over rows, 3x8–12 Biceps curls, 3x8–12 Wrist curls, 3x8–12

Figure 2-2. Sample workouts for developing pull-up strength in someone that can perform zero pull-ups in week 1 and can perform four pull-ups after 16 weeks of training

The Only Easy Day Was Yesterday

Chapter 1 covered the kinds of adaptations that the body makes from training. The problem is: the body doesn't "want" to adapt to training. It has to be dragged, kicking and screaming, to make those adaptations. The reason is that training-related adaptations are expensive, and the body avoids that at all costs. As a result, the body has to be convinced to continue to make adaptations from training. The only way this adaptation happens is if training becomes more difficult over time. Failing to do so means that gains stop. This is done by increasing the weight that is lifted, doing more repetitions, changing the rest between each set, and changing the exercises. Something must be done to make workouts more challenging in order for the body to keep making gains.

Figure 2-3 has a sample week of workouts. Figure 2-4 shows how these workouts can be modified to make them more difficult. Note that, in this example, each workout is modified a little differently to show the various ways that this increased difficulty can be accomplished.

Day 1	Day 2	Day 3	Day 4	Day 5
Back squats, 3x8x225 Lunges, 3x8x95 Romanian deadlifts, 3x8x225 Glute ham raises, 3x15x25 Standing calves, 3x12x200 Rest 2 minutes between sets.	Bench press, 3x6x200 Dips, 3x8x30 Military press, 3x8x95 Side raises, 3x15x15 Triceps extensions, 3x15x75 Rest 1 minute between sets.	Pull-ups, 3x8 Lat pulldowns, 3x8x150 Bent-over rows, 3x8x95 Barbell curls, 3x8x75 Wrist curls, 3x12x45 Rest 1 minute between sets.	Kettlebell swings, 3x8x35 Kettlebell snatch + overhead squats, 3x4+4x35 (each hand) Kettlebell clean + jerk, 3x4+4x35 (each hand) Windmills, 3x5x35 (each hand) Rest 1 minute between sets.	Heavy rope slams, 3x30 seconds Heavy rope one-handed slams, 3x30 seconds each hand Heavy rope circles, 3x30 seconds (clockwise, then counterclockwise) Heavy rope woodchoppers, 3x30 seconds Rest 1 minute between sets.
The notation is sets x repetitions x weight.				

Figure 2-3. Sample workouts

Day 1	Day 2	Day 3	Day 4	Day 5
Back squats, 3x4x265 Lunges, 3x4x120 Romanian deadlifts, 3x4x265 Glute ham raises, 3x12x35 Standing calves, 3x8x250 Rest 2 minutes between sets.	Bench press, 3x6x185 Dips, 3x8x20 Military press, 3x8x70 Side raises, 3x15x10 Triceps extensions, 3x15x45 Rest 30 seconds between sets.	Pull-ups, 3x15 Lat pulldowns, 3x15x120 Bent-over rows, 3x15x65 Barbell curls, 3x15x45 Wrist curls, 3x15x40 Rest 1 minute between sets.	Kettlebell one-handed swing + snatch + overhead squat, 3x(1+1+1x3) x25 Kettlebell clean + jerk + windmills, 3x(1+1+1x3) x25 Rest 1 minute between sets.	Circuit, perform each exercise for 30 seconds: Heavy rope slams Heavy rope one-handed slams Heavy rope circles (clockwise and counterclockwise) Heavy rope woodchoppers No rest, repeat circuit 3x.
The notation is sets x repetitions x weight.				

Figure 2-4. Examples of making the workouts in Figure 2-3 more difficult

Figure 2-4 has a few things to note. First, the weight was increased on day one. This weight increase causes the number of repetitions per set to decline dramatically. Second, the rest period was reduced on day two, which has the effect of lowering the amount of weight that can be lifted for a given number of repetitions. Third, the number of repetitions was increased on day three, which has the effect of reducing how much weight can be lifted. Fourth, the kettlebell exercises on day four are combined into supersets. This training is now executed faster, but is also more fatiguing, so the weight that can be lifted is decreased. Finally, on the last day, the workouts have been modified to be circuit-style, which means that the exercises are performed in order without rest, and then the entire circuit is repeated three times. Again, this approach is more tiring than performing all three sets of a given exercise and then moving on.

Pay Dues

It's natural to want to skip ahead to the point where an athlete is incredibly strong, fit, and can do all of the advanced workouts in this book. The problem is that this result takes time. Great strength, great fitness, and even the workouts in this book are based upon the assumption that athletes have paid their dues before getting to that point. It's important to build a foundation in terms of physical development and in terms of techniques as an athlete progresses through training. This helps an athlete to be able to withstand advanced training exercises and programs without becoming injured, and helps to maximize the effectiveness of those exercises. Failing to do so can increase the chances of getting injured and can lead to ineffective workouts. For example, an athlete wants to perform depth jumps in training. Depth jumps (i.e., dropping from a height and then jumping straight up into the air) are an advanced plyometric exercise that, while very effective at increasing power, requires the athlete to subject the lower body to an immense load.

To prepare for depth jumps, an athlete should master the techniques associated with landing safely as well as jumping. This mastery takes several months of training on plyometric exercises that teach both. In addition, the lower body should be prepared for loads it will sustain in the exercise through a progressive strength training routine that requires the lower body to become stronger and to adapt to the weights. Figure 2-5 shows a sample workout program to prepare an individual to be able to safely and effectively use depth jumps in a training session.

Effective strength and conditioning programs increase the athlete's performance and help to prevent injuries. Ineffective programs waste the athlete's time and may create bad movement patterns, develop bad habits, and contribute to injuries. With these aspects in mind, it is important to approach training in a methodical way to ensure that very little is left to chance.

	Day 1	Day 2	Day 3	Day 4	Day 5
Strength Training	Back squats, 3x8–12x80%	Power clean, 3x4–6x70%	Bench press, 3x8–12x80%	Front squats, 3x4–6x80%	Push jerk, 3x4–6x70%
	Lunges, 3x8-12	Clean pulls, 3x4–6x70%	Bent-over rows, 3x8–12	Reverse lunges, 3x8–12	Clean pulls, 3x4–6x70%
	Romanian deadlifts, 3x8–12	Kettlebell snatch, 3x6 each hand	Seated military press, 3x8–12	Good mornings, 3x8–12	Kettlebell swings, 3x6 each hand
	Glute ham raises, 3x15–20		Biceps/triceps 3x12–15 each	Reverse hyperextensions, 3x12-15	
	Calves, 3x15–20			Calves, 3x15–20	
Plyometrics		Squat jumps, 10x			Standing long jump, 10x
		Counter-movement jumps, 10x			Cone hops, 3x10 yards

Figure 2-5. Sample workout to build up the strength and technical ability to safely and effectively perform depth jumps

Chapter 3 How to Train Safely

Strength and conditioning has the potential to provide important benefits to an athlete. In order to get the benefits from training, it must be safe and athletes must stay injury-free. This chapter will cover the following concepts to help with training safely:

- Warming up
- Understanding when an athlete is hurt
- Staying safe

Warming Up

A good warm-up is important for preventing injuries and for maximizing performance. It prevents injuries by allowing the body to adjust to the demands of exercise gradually while also helping to make muscles, ligaments, and tendons more deformable through increased blood supply. It improves performance by cuing the nervous system, gradually providing a chance to increase focus, giving an opportunity to practice complex skills, and helping an athlete to recruit more muscle fibers. The warm-up also presents an opportunity to enhance fitness level and skill development. Ideally, this process should take anywhere between 10 and 30 minutes, depending upon fitness level, the workout that will follow, and the ambient conditions (e.g., extreme cold, extreme heat, etc.).

Several tools can be part of a successful warm-up:
- Cardio
- Mobility exercises
- Total body implements
- Prehab exercises
- Partial movements
- Light sets

After discussing the tools, this chapter will cover how to put everything together.

Cardio

Cardiovascular exercises are frequently used as warm-up. They have the benefit of raising heart rate, pumping blood throughout the body, and raising the temperature of muscles and joints. Some cardiovascular exercises focus on the lower body (stationary bicycles, ellipticals, steppers, jogging, and walking are examples), some exercises focus on the upper body (upper body ergometers and ellipticals), and some focus on both (ellipticals and swimming). When used as a warm-up, the idea is to elevate the heart rate, get blood moving, and get a light sweat going. This workout should not be exhaustive. Usually cardiovascular exercise would be done for around five minutes at a low to moderate intensity.

Mobility Exercises

Mobility exercises are designed to move the joint through its full range of motion. These are not classic stretching exercises in the sense that muscles are not maintained in a stretched position for a period of time. These exercises are focused around specific joints, muscles, and movement patterns and are typically performed for sets of 10 to 20 repetitions (or over 10 to 20 yards, depending on the exercise). They move the joint in a manner similar to how it will be used in training, get blood to the muscles and joint, and even help develop balance, coordination, and endurance. Categories of mobility exercises are listed in Figure 3-1.

Category of Exercise	Joint/Muscles Trained	Examples of Exercises
Ankle mobility drills	Ankle/calves	Ankle circles Walk on toes Jumping rope
Knee mobility drills	Knee/quadriceps	Heel kicks Kick the fence Lunges
Hamstring drills	Hamstrings	Marching Inchworms Backwards crab walk Kick the fence Lunges A drills
Hip mobility drills	Hip/glutes, hamstrings, quadriceps, hip flexors	Leg swings Eagles High-knee drills A drills B drills Lunges Kick the fence
Trunk mobility drills	Trunk/abdominals, erector spinae, hamstrings, hip flexors	Lunge + twist Marching (opposite hand to opposite foot) Woodchoppers Medicine ball throws
Shoulder mobility drills	Shoulders/deltoids, chest, upper back	Inchworms Arm circles Jumping rope Bear crawl

Figure 3-1. Sample mobility exercises

Total Body Implements

Total body movements using the heavy ropes, kettlebells, and strongman implements also make good warm-up exercises. Each of these tools can be used to train all of the muscles and joints of the body, can be done in rhythmical movements that also challenges the cardiovascular system, and serve as a great continuation of the effort begun with cardiovascular exercise. Total body exercises can be done for time (for example, swing the kettlebell for 30 seconds) and are very conducive to circuit training, which means a great deal of work can be done quickly.

Prehab Exercises

The concept of performing exercises to "prehab" joints (i.e., prevent injuries) is a recent one. These exercises are designed to address specific joints that are commonly injured; for example, exercises that address conditioning the lower back, ankles, and shoulders. These exercises involve a high volume (generally 15 to 20 repetitions) and are not done with much resistance. Usually one to two sets of these exercises are adequate, and they lend themselves to circuit-type training. Figure 3-2 has examples of prehab exercises.

Region Trained	Sample Exercises
Shoulder	Internal rotation External rotation Shoulder shrugs From all-fours: scapular protraction/retraction
Lower back	Prone back raises Prone arm raises Prone back raises Prone supermans Plank Side bridges
Ankle/shin	Walk on toes Walk on heels Walk, toes in Walk, toes out Stand on one foot

Figure 3-2. Sample prehab exercises

Partial Movements

Partial movements break up complicated movement patterns into their components. The idea is that practicing the components during the warm-up will help athletes to gradually increase focus and make athletes faster, stronger, and more explosive when they get to the main workout. Several types of exercises use partial movements, including the Olympic lifts, speed training, and agility training. These exercises are generally done with the same type of volume as the exercises they are training. For example, if an athlete is preparing for a speed training workout, then partial movements would consist of 10- to 20-yard drills. One to three sets is appropriate for these exercises, depending upon the nature of the upcoming workout.

Light Sets

In terms of strength training, the warm-up ends with light sets of the first exercise. The exercise begins with light sets that progressively increase in weight until the workout weight is reached. The idea is to gradually increase mental focus, recruit muscle fibers, and get the joints used to heavier weights. This should be done in a manner that prepares the body for the workout weights, but does not cause fatigue. This means that warm-up sets should be of low enough volume that they do not exhaust the athlete.

For example, if an athlete is going to do squats with 315 pounds for sets of six repetitions, then a warm-up might be as follows:
- Empty barbell: 12 repetitions
- 135 pounds: 12 repetitions
- 185 pounds: 8 repetitions
- 225 pounds: 4 repetitions
- 275 pounds: 2 repetitions
- 315 pounds: 6 repetitions

Putting Everything Together

Based upon the workout that will follow, the warm-up can be viewed as a series of steps. First, cardiovascular exercise is performed to begin the process, which is followed by total body implements. Any prehab exercises would be done next followed by either partial movements or light sets (as appropriate). Finally, the workout itself would begin. Two examples follow. The first is a warm-up for a metabolic conditioning workout that will use kettlebells, suspension training, and core training. The second is a warm-up for a total body strength training workout.

Example #1 (Metabolic Conditioning Workout)

This will be a very taxing metabolic conditioning workout that will be based around the following exercises:
- Kettlebell swings, snatches, cleans, jerks, overhead squats, get-ups
- Suspension rows, push-ups, flies, reverse flies, biceps curls, triceps extensions
- Crunches, sit-ups, cross-knee crunches, lying leg raises, flutter kicks, planks

The workout will proceed as follows:
- Kettlebell swings
- Suspension rows

- Crunches
- Kettlebell snatches
- Suspension push-ups
- Sit-ups
- Kettlebell cleans
- Suspension flies
- Cross-knee crunches
- Kettlebell jerks
- Suspension reverse flies
- Lying leg raises
- Kettlebell overhead squats
- Suspension biceps curls
- Flutter kicks
- Kettlebell get-ups
- Suspension triceps extensions
- Planks

Each exercise will be performed for 20 seconds, and the entire circuit will be repeated three times with two minutes rest between each circuit. The entire circuit should take about 22 minutes to complete.

To prepare for this workout, the warm-up will consist of cardio and mobility exercises. The warm-up will begin with a slow 400-meter jog, which will be followed with five minutes of jump roping. Next, the following mobility exercises will be done to help prepare for the workout: ankle circles, leg swings, eagles, arm circles, bear crawls, and push-ups. Each mobility exercise will be done for 15 to 20 repetitions.

Example #2 (Strength Training Workout)

This will be a full body strength training workout based around the following exercises:
- Power snatch
- Back squats
- Romanian deadlifts
- Bench press
- Bent-over rows

The power snatch will be done for five sets of three repetitions at 70 percent of maximum (5x3x70%). Back squats and bench press will be done for 3x4–8x85%. Romanian deadlifts and bent over rows will be done for 3x8x~80%.

To prepare for this workout, cardio, mobility exercises, partial movements, and light sets will be used. The warm-up will begin with five minutes on the stationary bike.

After that, the following mobility exercises will be done to help prepare for the workout: ankle circles, leg swings, eagles, arm circles, bear crawls, and push-ups. Each mobility exercise will be done for 15 to 20 repetitions. Following the mobility exercises, the following partial movements will be done to prepare for the power snatch: snatch grip shrugs, snatch grip upright rows, muscle snatches, and overhead squats. Each will be done three to four times with just the barbell. Next, the warm-up will conclude with light sets of the power snatch. In this example, the athlete's maximum in the power snatch is 100 kg, so the workout will consist of 5x3x70kg. With this in mind, the light sets will look as follows:

- 1x3x20kg (e.g., the barbell)
- 1x3x40kg
- 1x3x50kg
- 1x3x60kg

Understanding When an Athlete Is Hurt

It's normal to be sore after a good workout, especially if an athlete has made a change to the workout (e.g., increased the weight, added a new exercise, etc.). However, one of the consequences of pushing the body is that the body may not heal quickly enough, and an injury could eventually develop. Recognizing injuries, learning how to train around them, and learning when not to train are important skills for anyone on a serious training program.

Recognizing Common Injuries

Since this book is not about contact sports, the discussion will be focused on injuries that either occur to weak links (such as soft tissue) or injuries that happen as a result of too much work being done too soon (e.g., overuse injuries).

Two common types of injuries are strains and sprains. Sprains occur when a ligament (which attaches bone to bone) is overstretched. This injury can range in severity from the ligament is just overly stretched and sore all the way to the ligament is completely torn. Strains are the stretching or tearing of a muscle or tendon. Again, this can range from soreness to a complete tear. Sprains and strains result in pain, and as they become more serious, they may result in loss of function and swelling. The lower levels of severity will heal by themselves; more complete tears may require surgery to fix. Some of these injuries can be trained around, others cannot. This will depend upon the severity and the location of the strain/sprain.

Areas that are commonly injured from aggressive training programs include:
- *Shoulders:* The shoulder is a common area of injury. The most common shoulder injury that results from training is an injury relating to the rotator cuff, which is a group of small muscles that help attach the arm to the trunk. If any of these

muscles become inflamed, then it can cause them to be pushed up against bone or ligaments. This type of injury can also result from a repetitive overhead motion where tendons are caught between the humerus and scapula.

- *Elbows:* Elbow injuries from training are usually a result of overstressing the biceps (from heavy curls, heavy pull-ups, and rows), overstressing the triceps tendon (from heavy presses or dips), or overstressing the ligaments that connect the humerus to the ulna.
- *Lower back:* Lower back injuries range in severity from strains and sprains of the muscles and ligaments that act on the lumbar vertebrae all the way to damage to the discs that separate the lumbar vertebrae. A severe enough injury can cause the material of the disc to push out against the spinal cord and nerves, causing pain and muscle spasms.
- *Hamstrings:* Hamstring strains are a common injury, usually associated with sprinting. This injury will limit an athlete's ability to sprint, jump, change directions, and squat below a certain depth.
- *Knees:* Knee injuries that are common from training include strains to the patellar tendon, strains to the quadriceps tendon, and sprains to the various collateral ligaments. These injuries all can be from chronic overuse or from an improper change of direction or landing.
- *Shins:* Injuries to the shin are usually a result of not adjusting to training volume, footwear, training surfaces, or all of the above. They can range from mild soreness during activity, to extreme soreness all the time, to stress fractures in the tibia.

What to Do About Injuries

Injuries do happen as a result of training. If this happens, options include the following:
- *Ignore it:* For small problems, this is a viable option, but for obvious reasons it's not an option that is recommended. Ignoring injuries has a tendency to make them worse so that small, annoying problems can become big and debilitating.
- *Seek medical attention:* This can be a frustrating option because, unless it is a really severe injury, most medical doctors will recommend taking time off and anti-inflammatories for many of the injuries described.
- *Take time off:* If left alone, many of the injuries described will heal within two to eight weeks unless they are more severe in nature (severe strain/sprain, lumbar disc herniation, etc.). If an injury doesn't resolve in two to eight weeks, this is an indication that medical attention is necessary.
- *Train around it:* Injuries can be trained around. This means determining what aggravates the injury and then modifying exercises so that the injury isn't aggravated. This allows for an athlete to maintain their fitness level while letting the injury heal. For example, while deep squats will aggravate a hamstring injury, quarter squats may not. While the quarter squat may not be ideal, it allows for some fitness and strength to be maintained while letting the hamstrings heal.

Staying Safe

In addition to avoiding injuries and taking them seriously when they occur, athletes can do a number of other things to stay safe while training. These include the following:

- Unclutter the facility.
- Learn good technique.
- Start slowly.
- Use the athletic stance.

Unclutter the Facility

An easily avoidable cause of injuries from working out is caused by cluttered training facilities. One of the most common causes of injury is from tripping over equipment that has been left on the floor. The following are principles for keeping a facility safe:

- If it's not being used, put it where it belongs. Barbells, dumbbells, kettlebells, and other assorted training tools are great tripping hazards.
- Rack the weights. Weight plates are another great tripping hazard. It's also a good idea to put the weight plates where they belong so they are easy to find (i.e., put the 25-pound plates together, not mixed in with the 5s and 45s).
- Give barbells enough space. A barbell ideally should have two feet of clearance on either side. This is to prevent anyone from bumping the bar during the lift and it also gives people room in case the plates fall off the bar.
- Stay off the platform when others are training the Olympic lifts. A person performing the Olympic lifts needs an 8 x 8 foot space to do so. This gives plenty of room for the bar, split lifts, and moving around with a difficult lift. Standing too close to the lifter cramps them and increases the odds of the barbell hitting the person standing too close.
- Stay away from the mirror during kettlebell lifts. Even people that are very strong get sweaty, tired, and lose their grip during kettlebell exercises. Performing the lifts near the mirror is inviting a broken mirror.

Learn Good Techniques

A more subtle cause of injuries from training is bad technique. Bad technique effects how joints, ligaments, tendons, and muscles are loaded. For example, allowing the shoulders to round forward while performing back squats unevenly distributes the load across the lumbar vertebrae, possibly setting someone up for a lower back injury. In each part of this book, conditioning programs are designed to build upon the one that came before it. This is to allow athletes to master fundamental techniques and build the necessary fitness base before attempting more advanced exercises.

Start Slowly

Fatigue is a part of any kind of training. Eventually, as athletes become more fit, they can function at higher levels while fatigued. Lifting heavy weights is generally a desired goal with training, but as athletes get closer to their potential, sacrifices have to be made in terms of technique to lift heavier weights. It takes time to develop the fitness base to be able to achieve these things safely and effectively. For example, the section of this book that covers the deadlift exercise will discuss how it should be performed with the chest out and shoulders pulled back to protect that back. In addition, while lifting the barbell off the floor; the hips, knees, and shoulders should move at the same speed. However, elite powerlifters making maximal lifts in competition don't lift like this, they make many technical mistakes, including rounding their shoulders forward and allowing their hips to rise faster than their shoulders—both of which are potentially dangerous for the lower back. Because they have spent years getting their body in shape, they are able to do this without crippling themselves—but this process takes time to do.

Use the Athletic Stance

A lot of the exercises in this book begin from the athletic stance. In this position, an athlete is balanced and primed to move explosively in any direction. To get into stance, the athlete should stand up tall with the feet hip-width apart. The athlete should pull the shoulders back and stick the chest out. From this position, the athlete should push the hips back, unlocking the knees. The hips should be pushed back until there is an approximate 135-degree angle at the knees. The athlete should keep the weight on the balls of the feet. Figure 3-3 shows what this position looks like.

Figure 3-3. The athletic stance

Exercise should be fun and effective. In order for that to be the case, it has to be done in a safe manner that allows for an athlete to remain injury-free. Warming up adequately, honestly recognizing when an athlete is hurt, and taking simple steps to stay safe will go a long way to making this a positive and rewarding experience.

Part II TOOLS

The second part of this book consists of six chapters that introduce many of the tools that are used in modern strength and conditioning. These tools include free weights, kettlebells, suspension training, heavy ropes, sandbag training, and speed/agility/plyometrics. Today, these are all tools that an entry-level strength and conditioning coach is expected to have mastered, and they are something that all athletic coaches and athletes will encounter.

Each chapter is organized around a specific tool and introduces a group of core exercises. For example, Chapter 5 focuses on kettlebell exercises, including swings, cleans, snatches, jerks, get-ups, and windmills. Each exercise is described and extensively illustrated. When it is appropriate, learning progressions and variations are also included for the exercises.

Each tool has many possible exercises for which it can be used. The focus of this book is to ensure that the athlete's time is used most effectively during training. As a result, this book is focusing on those exercises that each tool performs best in an athletic strength and conditioning setting. For example, an athlete can perform a bench press with a heavy rope, but a barbell will be a much more effective way to address that exercise.

Chapter 4 Free Weights

Free weights are a great tool for increasing muscle mass, increasing strength, and improving power. These exercises generally form the foundation of any athletic strength and conditioning program. This chapter is going to focus on the following exercises:

- Squats
- Hip extension exercises
- Presses
- Rows/pulls
- Power cleans
- Power snatches
- Jerks

Squats

Squats are one of the most essential kinds of exercise for athletes to perform. They are performed standing up, involve exerting force against the ground, develop the muscles of the trunk and lower body, and are important for increasing bone strength. This chapter is going to cover several squat variations:

- Back squats
- Front squats
- Split squats
- Overhead squats
- Pause/eccentric squats
- Squats with bands and chains

Back Squats

Back squats train the muscles that act on the hips, knees, and ankles. They also develop the muscles that act on the spine and strengthen pretty much every bone that is beneath the barbell. This exercise is performed in a manner similar to how many activities in real life are performed, so the thinking is that it has a lot of transfer to the playing field as well as activities of daily life.

To perform the back squat, the athlete should stand up with the barbell on the back of the shoulders. It should rest in a position that is comfortable. If training for a specific goal (like powerlifting, Olympic lifting, etc.), then this goal may alter the bar's positioning on the back. But for most athletes, it just needs to be in a comfortable position. The athlete should stick the chest out and pull the shoulders back; this positioning is called setting the back. This position should be maintained throughout the exercise. Feet should be between hip-width apart and shoulder-width apart, wherever comfortable (Figure 4-1). From this position, keeping the weight on the heels, the hips should be pushed back while allowing the knees to bend. The athlete should lower himself until the thighs are parallel to the floor (Figure 4-2). Next, the athlete should reverse directions until he is standing straight up. This process should be repeated for the desired number of repetitions.

Figure 4-1. Back squat—starting position

Figure 4-2. Back squat—descent

Front Squats

Front squats also train the muscles that act on the hips, knees, and ankles. This exercise requires the lifter to be more upright than in the back squat, so it also emphasizes the muscles of the trunk. Like back squats, this is the kind of exercise that should have a great deal of transfer to the playing field as well as activities of daily life.

The athlete should stand in front of the barbell and grip it with a shoulder-width grip, and the palms should face down. As the athlete steps under the barbell, the elbows should rotate as they move from behind the barbell to in front of the barbell. If done correctly, the barbell will be resting on the front of the shoulders with the elbows high (the upper arm should be parallel to the floor) (Figure 4-3). From this position, the athlete should step back with the barbell on the front of the shoulders and the back set. The feet should be placed between hip-width and shoulder-width apart with the weight should be on the heels (Figure 4-4). While keeping the upper arms parallel to the floor, the athlete should push the hips back and bend the knees while descending into the squat. Note that, due to the need to keep the trunk upright, this exercise is more knee-dominant than the back squat. The athlete should squat down as far as is comfortable, keeping the upper arms parallel to the floor (Figure 4-5), and then reverse directions until standing straight up. Have the athlete repeat for the desired number of repetitions.

Figure 4-3. Front squat—racking the barbell

Figure 4-4. Front squat—starting position

Figure 4-5. Front squat—descent

Split Squats

Split squats offer many of the benefits of the back squat, but they allow athletes to focus on one leg more than the other. For a number of activities in daily life and sports, one leg does more work than the other. For example, when running only one leg is in contact with the ground at a time. Only one leg kicks a ball. When throwing, athletes tend to lever off one leg.

To perform split squats, have the athlete stand up with the barbell on the back of the shoulders. It should rest in a position that is comfortable. The back should be set. For this exercise, the athlete needs to take a big step back with one leg. The step should be far enough back so that the heel of the back foot is off the ground (i.e., only the toes and ball of the back foot are in contact with the ground) (Figure 4-6). From this position, the athlete will descend, using the front leg. As this is being done, the back knee needs to be bent. The descent should be to a point where the front thigh is parallel to the ground (Figure 4-7). Note that the back knee should not touch the ground. Using mostly the front leg, the athlete will reverse directions until back in the starting position. Have the athlete repeat for the desired number of repetitions, and then switch legs.

Figure 4-6. Split squat—starting position

Figure 4-7. Split squat—descent

Overhead Squats

Overhead squats offer many of the benefits of the back squat, but they also increase the mobility of the hips and knees as well as developing the muscles of the trunk and shoulder. This exercise is challenging to manage as more skill and balance are involved in performing this exercise compared to other squat variations.

To perform overhead squats, have the athlete stand up with the barbell on the back of the shoulders. The back should be set. Using a snatch-width grip on the barbell, the athlete should press the bar overhead.

In this position, the bar should be directly in line with the hips, with the arms next to the ears. The feet should be between hip-width apart and shoulder-width apart, with the weight on the heels (Figure 4-8). Keeping the elbows locked out, the athlete should push the hips back and allow the knees to bend while squatting down as far as is comfortable (Figure 4-9). The barbell must remain over the hips, with the elbows straight, for this exercise to be executed successfully. The athlete should then reverse directions until he is back in the starting position. Have the athlete repeat for the desired number of repetitions.

Figure 4-8. Overhead squat—starting position

Figure 4-9. Overhead squat—descent

Pause/Eccentric Squats

Pause squats are an advanced training tool that can be used to enhance any of the types of squats that have been described in this chapter. Pause squats are designed to help strengthen the ability to get out of the bottom position in the squat. This exercise is performed exactly like any of the squat variations covered—with two important differences: pause for a full count in the bottom position, and then attempt to ascend as quickly as possible.

Eccentric squats are another advanced exercise that helps to strengthen lowering the barbell. They are performed like any of the squat variations covered—with one important difference: the descent needs to be exaggerated. For example, the athlete should take 10 slow seconds to descend, and then come out of the bottom position as quickly as possible.

Normally, both of these exercises are done for sets of no more than four to six repetitions with weights around 60 to 80 percent of the weights that would have been used on the regular exercise. Both exercises are extremely tiring, this is why the number of repetitions and the amount of weight needs to be restricted. When performing these exercises, it is important to focus on good technique (chest out, shoulders back, weight on heels, etc.) as the tiring nature of the exercises can lead to bad technique and possible injury.

Squats With Bands and Chains

Bands and chains are both advanced tools designed to strengthen specific phases of the squat. These tools can be used in conjunction with any of the types of squats that have been described in this chapter. Bands are essentially large rubber bands that are looped around the ends of the barbell and attached either to the floor or a height (Figure 4-10). When they are attached to the floor, they shorten as the descent phase of the squat is performed. As this movement is reversed, they stretch out as the lifter

Figure 4-10. Bands

ascends out of the squat. The more the lifter ascends, the more stretched out the bands become. As the bands stretch out, they resist further stretch. In other words, they make it more difficult to stand up from a squat. When they are suspended from a height, they stretch out as the lifter descends into the squat and shorten as the lifter stands up. In other words, they make it more difficult for a lifter to descend. These are meant to address specific weaknesses, which is why they should only be used by advanced individuals.

Chains are long chain links that are suspended from the barbell and hang down toward the floor. As the lifter descends into the squat, the chain links begin to accumulate on the floor. This serves to reduce the amount of weight on the barbell (because the chain links are being supported by the floor). As the lifter ascends from the bottom position, the links leave the floor and are supported by the barbell. This technique serves to increase the weight on the barbell, making the lift more difficult. This tool is also meant to address specific weaknesses during the squat and should be used by advanced individuals.

Hip Extension Exercises

Hip extension exercises address three groups of muscles: the lower back muscles, the glutes, and the hamstrings. These are important muscles to strengthen in movements that make them work together because these muscles are key to jumping, sprinting, and agility. In addition, these exercises address strengthening these muscles (particularly the hamstrings) while they are lengthened, which will go a long way toward preventing injuries. This chapter is going to focus on the following exercises:

- Deadlifts
- Romanian deadlifts
- Good mornings—standing
- Good mornings—seated
- Back raises
- Reverse hyperextensions
- Glute-ham raises

Deadlifts

Deadlifts are a hip extension exercise that trains the majority of the muscles of the body. Like squats, they involve extension of the hips and knees while exerting force against the ground. Unlike squats, deadlifts are about lifting the barbell off the floor.

Deadlifts begin with the barbell on the floor. The athlete should approach the barbell with the feet hip-width apart. The athlete needs to set the back and maintain this position throughout the exercise. In the starting position, the athlete will squat until the hands can grip the barbell. The deadlift is generally performed with a mixed grip on the bar (i.e., one hand facing away, one had facing toward) with the hands shoulder-width apart and the arms straight. If done properly, the shoulders will be slightly ahead of the barbell (Figure 4-11). From this position, the athlete will extend the hips and knees, lifting the barbell off the floor. As the barbell reaches mid-thigh height, the hips should be extended so that the body straightens up (Figure 4-12). The barbell is then lowered, the athlete resets, and the desired number of repetitions is performed.

Figure 4-11. Deadlift—starting position

Figure 4-12. Deadlift—ending position

One variation of this exercise is to perform "sumo" deadlifts. This option involves having the feet wider than shoulder-width apart (Figure 4-13). Because of the greater foot width, more emphasis is placed on using the legs (rather than the back) to lift the weight.

Figure 4-13. Sumo deadlift

Romanian Deadlifts

The Romanian deadlift primarily focuses on the hamstrings, glutes, and lower back muscles. To perform this exercise, the athlete will stand up with the barbell in the hands. The hands should be shoulder-width apart, and the arms should be straight. The athlete's feet should be hip-width apart. It is important that the athlete set the back (Figure 4-14). Keeping the knees soft and arms straight, the hips should be pushed back. As the hips are pushed back, the athlete will lean forward and allow the bar to travel down the legs, keeping it close to the legs throughout. The athlete should lean forward as far as flexibility allows (Figure 4-15). Have the athlete reverse direction and repeat for the desired number of repetitions.

Figure 4-14. Romanian deadlifts—starting position

Figure 4-15. Romanian deadlifts—descent

Good Mornings—Standing

Standing good mornings mimic the movement patterns of the Romanian deadlift, but the barbell is on the back of the shoulders instead of in the hands. This exercise develops the muscles of the glutes, hamstrings, and lower back. Standing good mornings are performed by standing up with the barbell on the back of the shoulders. The athlete's feet should be hip-width apart, and the back should be set. Like with Romanian deadlifts, the exercise is performed by keeping the knees soft and pushing the hips back. As the hips are pushed back, the athlete will lean forward as far as flexibility comfortably allows (Figure 4-16). Have the athlete reverse directions and repeat for the desired number of repetitions.

Figure 4-16. Standing good mornings—descent position

Good Mornings—Seated

Seated good mornings are good mornings performed from a seated position. Often, this exercise is less stressful to the lower back than the standing variation. To perform this exercise, have the athlete sit down on a bench with the barbell on the back of the shoulders. The legs should straddle the bench with the feet flat on the ground. After setting the back, have the athlete lean forward as far as flexibility allows (Figure 4-17). Have the athlete reverse directions and repeat for the desired number of repetitions.

Figure 4-17. Seated good mornings—descent position

Back Raises

Back raises are an exercise that trains the muscles of the lower back, glutes, and hamstrings. They do not require as much technique as the Romanian deadlifts and good mornings. To perform this exercise, the athlete will approach the back raise bench. The athlete should get on the bench so that the body lies face down. The ankles should be secured by the ankle pads. It is important that the hips are well forward of the thigh pads to allow for a full range of motion. The legs should be straight. The athlete should set the back and place the hands where they are comfortable. Moving from the hips, the exercise is performed by lowering the upper body as far down as flexibility will allow (Figure 4-18). Using the hamstrings, the upper body is lifted until it is parallel to the floor. Have the athlete lower and repeat for the desired number of repetitions. To add resistance to this exercise, a weight can be held across the chest or behind the head.

Figure 4-18. Back raises—descent position

Reverse Hyperextensions

Reverse hyperextensions are another tool for developing the muscles of the lower back, hamstrings, and glutes. To perform, the athlete should lie face down on the back raise bench. The body should be positioned so that the hips and legs are suspended in the air and the hips are flexed to a 90-degree angle. The athlete's arms should reach forward, and the hands should grab the ankle pads on the back raise bench, securing the upper body while performing this exercise (Figure 4-19). Keeping the legs straight and together, the athlete should raise the legs up until they are parallel to the ground (see Figure 4-20). Have the athlete lower, and repeat for the desired number of repetitions.

Figure 4-19. Reverse hyperextensions—starting position

Figure 4-20. Reverse hyperextensions—top position

Glute-Ham Raises

Glute-ham raises are a more advanced exercise than the back raise, but they are extremely effective at strengthening the hamstrings, glutes, and lower back. To perform this exercise, the athlete will lie face down in the glute-ham raise bench, with the ankles secured under the ankle pads. The ankle pads should be adjusted so that the hips are on the hip pads (Figure 4-21). From this position, keeping the body as straight as possible, the athlete will perform the exercise by pushing the knees down so that they touch the knee pads. As the knees touch the knee pads, the upper body will be lifted up, using the hamstrings until the body is making a 90-degree angle with the ground (Figure 4-22). Have the athlete lower under control and repeat for the desired number of repetitions.

Figure 4-21. Glute-ham raises—starting position

Figure 4-22. Glute-ham raises—ending position

Presses

Presses are multi-joint movements that develop the muscles of the chest, shoulders, and triceps. These muscles are important for making contact with opponents, pushing them, and throwing. While many of these movements are not performed in a sport-specific position, the exercises offer the potential for transfer to many activities. This chapter will cover the following exercises:

- Bench press
- Incline press
- Decline press
- Dips
- Military press

Bench Press

The bench press develops the chest, shoulders, and triceps. While lying on a bench, the athlete holds the barbell above the face or chest at arm's length, brings it down to the chest, then presses it back up. To perform the bench press, have the athlete lie face-up on the bench. The head, shoulders, and hips should be in contact with the bench throughout the exercise. Ideally, the feet should be flat on the floor. The body should be positioned so that the eyes are directly under the barbell when it is on the bench's uprights. The athlete should grip the bar with a shoulder-width grip, extend the arms, lift the bar off the uprights, and bring the bar so that it is over the chest (Figure 4-23). From this position, the barbell should be lowered until it touches the lower half of the chest (Figure 4-24). Without bouncing the bar, the athlete should press the bar up until the arms are straight and the barbell is back above the chest. Have the athlete repeat for the desired number of repetitions.

Figure 4-23. Bench press—starting position

Figure 4-24. Bench press—descent

Incline Press

The incline press is performed on a bench that is angled so that the upper body is higher than the hips. This kind of variation emphasizes the clavicular part of the chest and the shoulders more than the bench press, which also means that less weight can be lifted than in the bench press. To perform this exercise, the athlete will lie face-up on the bench. The head, shoulders, and hips should be in contact with the bench throughout the exercise. Ideally, the feet should be flat on the floor. Have the athlete grip the bar with a shoulder-width grip. Next, the athlete should extend the arms, lifting the bar off the uprights, and bring the bar forward until it is positioned over the chest (Figure 4-25). The bar should be lowered to a point just below the clavicles, touching the chest with the bar (Figure 4-26). Without bouncing the bar off the chest, the athlete will reverse direction and press it up until the arms are straight and the barbell is back above the chest. Have the athlete repeat for the desired number of repetitions.

Figure 4-25. Incline press—starting position

Figure 4-26. Incline press—descent

Decline Press

The decline press is performed on a bench that is angled so that the upper body is lower than the hips. This kind of variation shortens the distance that the barbell travels during the press, which can make it easier for many people to perform. The decline press is performed by lying face-up on the bench. The head, shoulders, and hips should be in contact with the bench throughout the exercise. The athlete should secure the ankles behind the ankle pads. The athlete will grip the bar with a shoulder-width grip, extend the arms, lift the bar off the uprights, and bring the bar until it is over the chest (Figure 4-27). Next, the bar should be lowered until it touches the lower half of the chest (Figure 4-28). Without bouncing the bar, the athlete should reverse direction and press it up until the arms are straight and the barbell is back above the chest. Have the athlete repeat for the desired number of repetitions.

Figure 4-27. Decline press—starting position

Figure 4-28. Decline press—finish

Dips

Dips are a great bodyweight exercise for training the muscles of the chest, shoulders, and triceps. To perform dips, have the athlete grab the dip bars with an overhand grip. The athlete should jump up and begin this exercise on extended arms, with the feet off the ground (Figure 4-29). The athlete should lean forward slightly and allow the arms to flex, lowering the upper body until the upper arms are parallel to the floor (Figure 4-30). Have the athlete reverse direction and repeat for the desired number of repetitions.

Figure 4-29. Dips—starting position

Figure 4-30. Dips—ending position

Military Press

The military press is an exercise primarily for the shoulders and the triceps. It can be performed standing or seated. The standing variation is performed by standing up with the barbell on the front of the shoulders and the feet hip-width apart. Taking a shoulder-width grip on the barbell, the athlete should grip the barbell so that the palms face away from the body. It is important for the athlete to set the back. From this position, the barbell should be pressed up and slightly behind the head. The bar should move in a path so that it ends up in line with the hips while overhead (Figure 4-31). Have the athlete lower the bar and repeat for the desired number of repetitions.

Figure 4-31. Standing military press—ending position

The military press can also be performed from a seated position. It is performed in the same manner as the standing variation (i.e., chest out, shoulders back, press the bar up, bar ends up in line with the hips) with the exception that foot placement is not as important as with the standing variation.

Note that the bench press, incline press, decline press, and military press can all be performed with barbells (which is described) and also with dumbbells.

Rows/Pulls

Rows and pulls are exercises that target the muscles of the upper back, the shoulders, and the biceps. These muscles are important for running, posture, and for throwing. In addition, addressing these muscles can help to prevent shoulder injuries that may be caused by strength imbalances at the shoulder joint. This chapter will cover the following rows/pulls:

- Bent-over rows
- One-arm dumbbell rows
- Pull-ups
- Shrugs

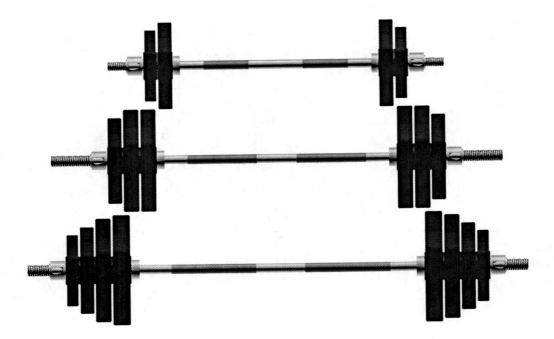

Bent-Over Rows

Bent-over rows are one of the primary exercises for the muscles of the upper back. To perform bent-over rows, the athlete should stand up with the barbell in their hands. Feet should be hip-width apart. Hands should grip the bar with an overhand grip, with the hands shoulder-width apart. The athlete should set the back. Keeping the arms straight and knees soft, the athlete should push the hips back and allow the barbell to slide down along the thighs. The barbell should be held close to the thighs (Figure 4-32). While keeping the elbows close to the body, the athlete should pull the barbell toward the stomach (Figure 4-33). Have the athlete lower and repeat for the desired number of repetitions.

Figure 4-32. Bent-over rows—starting position

Figure 4-33. Bent-over rows—ending position

One-Arm Dumbbell Rows

One-arm dumbbell rows allows for each side of the body to be developed independently while minimizing the stress on the lower back. To perform this exercise, have the athlete place a dumbbell on the floor, on the right side of a bench. The athlete will then place the left hand, knee, and shin on the bench. The left arm should be straight. The athlete should grip the dumbbell in the right hand and set the back (Figure 4-34). Without swinging, the athlete will pull the dumbbell toward the right side of the body at stomach level. The athlete should keep the elbow close to the body (Figure 4-35). Have the athlete lower and repeat for the desired number of repetitions, then switch sides.

Figure 4-34. One-arm dumbbell rows—starting position

Figure 4-35. One-arm dumbbell rows—ending position

Pull-Ups

Pull-ups are another exercise that trains the muscles of the upper back, shoulder, and biceps. They take time to master, but the benefits are worth the investment. This exercise may be performed as a chin-up or as a pull-up.

Chin-Ups

Chin-ups are performed by approaching the pull-up bar and gripping the bar with a slightly narrower than shoulder-width grip. Gripping the pull-up bar with an underhanded grip, the athlete will hang down from the pull-up bar so that the arms are fully extended (Figure 4-36). Drawing the shoulder blades together, the athlete should flex the elbows so that the head and chin is pulled over the bar (Figure 4-37). Have the athlete lower and repeat for the desired number of repetitions.

Figure 4-36. Chin-ups— starting position

Figure 4-37. Chin-ups— ending position

Pull-Ups

To perform pull-ups, the athlete should approach the pull-up bar and grip it with a wider than shoulder-width grip. The pull-up bar should be gripped with an overhand grip. The athlete will then hang down from the pull-up bar so that the arms are fully extended (Figure 4-38). Drawing the shoulder blades together, the athlete should flex the elbows so that the head and chin is pulled over the bar (Figure 4-39). Have the athlete lower and repeat for the desired number of repetitions.

Figure 4-38. Pull-ups—starting position

Figure 4-39. Pull-ups—ending position

Shrugs

Shrugs develop the muscles of the traps and the neck. They can be performed with barbells, dumbbells, and kettlebells. This chapter will cover barbell shrugs, but the same technique is easily adapted to the other implements.

To perform barbell shrugs, the athlete will approach the bar and take an overhand, shoulder-width grip on the bar. The athlete should stand up with the barbell in the hands. The arms should be straight, and the back should be set (Figure 4-40). Keeping the arms straight, the athlete will lift the shoulders up as high as they will go (Figure 4-41). Have the athlete lower and repeat for the desired number of repetitions.

Figure 4-40. Shrugs—starting position

Figure 4-41. Shrugs—ending position

Power Cleans

The power clean is a total body exercise that involves lifting the barbell from the floor to the shoulders in one movement. It is a staple of athletic strength and conditioning programs because it is performed standing up, is explosive in nature, and is relatively easy to learn. This chapter will cover three variations of this lift:

- Power cleans
- Power cleans from the hang
- Clean pulls

Power Cleans

Power cleans are performed with the barbell on the floor. To perform the power clean, the athlete should approach the barbell. Feet should be hip-width apart. Keeping the arms straight and the feet flat on the ground, the athlete should squat down and grip the barbell with an overhand grip. Hands should be shoulder-width apart. It is important for the athlete to set the back and maintain this position throughout the exercise. The athlete should adjust the height of the hips so that the shoulders are ahead of the barbell (Figure 4-42). From the starting position, the athlete should extend the hips and knees, slowly pulling the barbell off the ground. As the bar reaches mid-thigh level, the athlete should explosively extend the hips, knees, and ankles while shrugging the shoulders up (Figure 4-43). The athlete must allow the barbell to move up the body, and as the bar reaches shoulder height, the athlete should drop under the bar into a quarter squat. The athlete will receive the bar on the front of the shoulders with the elbows high (Figure 4-44). From that position, the athlete should stand up, lower the bar, then repeat for the desired number of repetitions.

Figure 4-42. Power clean—starting position

Figure 4-43. Power clean—explosion

Figure 4-44. Power clean—receiving the barbell

Power Cleans From the Hang

The power clean can also be performed from a position where the barbell does not start on the floor, but is supported by the body. This is called a power clean from the hang. These variations are easier to learn, but often result in less weight being lifted. The three principal variations of the power clean from the hang each refer to the starting position of the barbell:

- Power clean—hang—above the knee
- Power clean—hang—knee
- Power clean—hang—below the knee

Power Clean—Hang—Above the Knee

To perform the power clean from the hang, with the bar above the knees, the athlete should stand up with the barbell in his hands. The athlete will take a power clean grip on the bar and set the back. Keeping the knees soft, the athlete should push the hips back to get into the starting position. As the hips are pushed back, the athlete should allow the barbell to slide down along the thighs until it is at mid-thigh level. This is the starting position (Figure 4-45). From this point, the athlete will perform the explosion as described and receive the bar on the front of the shoulders. Have the athlete lower and repeat for the desired number of repetitions.

Figure 4-45. Power clean—hang—above the knee—starting position

Power Clean—Hang—Knee

To perform the power clean from the hang, with the bar at the knees, the athlete will stand up with the barbell in his hands. Using a clean grip on the bar, the athlete will set the back and assume the same starting position as the power clean, hang, above the knee variation described. From this position, the athlete will continue pushing the hips back and bending the knees until the bar is at knee level. The shoulders should be ahead of the bar in this position. This is the starting position (Figure 4-46). Fromthis point, the athlete will slowly lift the bar around the knees, perform the explosion as described, and receive the bar on the front of the shoulders. Have the athlete lower and repeat for the desired number of repetitions.

Figure 4-46. Power clean—hang—knee—starting position

Power Clean—Hang—Below the Knee

To perform the power clean from the hang, with the bar below the knees, the athlete will get into the same starting position described in the power clean, hang, knee variation described. From this point, the athlete will continue pushing the hips back and bending the knees until the bar is below knee level. The shoulders should be ahead of the bar in this position. This is the starting position (Figure 4-47). From this point, the athlete will slowly lift the bar around the knees, perform the explosion as described, and receive the bar on the front of the shoulders. Have the athlete lower and repeat for the desired number of repetitions.

Figure 4-47. Power clean—hang—below the knee—starting position

Clean Pulls

The clean pull is a partial movement that has all the benefits of the power clean but involves less technique. This exercise can be performed from the floor or from any of the hang positions. This exercise is performed just like the power clean except that it stops after the explosion (i.e., there is no quarter squat, and the barbell is not brought to the shoulders).

Power Snatches

The power snatch is a total body exercise that involves lifting the weight from the floor to overhead in one motion. It is also widely used in athletic strength and conditioning programs, though it can be more challenging to learn than the power clean. This chapter will cover three variations of this lift:

- Power snatches with barbell on floor
- Power snatches from the hang
- Snatch pulls

Power Snatches With Barbell on Floor

Power snatches are performed with the barbell on the floor. To perform the power snatch, the athlete should approach the barbell. With the feet hip-width apart, the athlete will squat down and grip the barbell with an overhand grip, keeping the arms straight. The hands should be wider than shoulder-width apart. It is important for the athlete to set the back and to maintain this position throughout the exercise. The athlete should adjust the height of the hips so that the shoulders are ahead of the barbell. This is the starting position (Figure 4-48). From this point, the athlete should extend the hips and knees, slowly pulling the barbell off the ground. As the bar reaches a point just below the hips, the athlete will explosively extend their hips and knees while moving up onto their toes and shrugging their shoulders up (Figure 4-49). The athlete should allow the barbell to move up the body. As the bar reaches shoulder height, the athlete should drop under the bar into a quarter squat. As the athlete moves into the squat, the bar should be received overhead on fully extended arms. Done properly, the bar should be slightly behind the head so that it is directly in line with the hips (Figure 4-50). After receiving the bar, the athlete will stand up, lower the barbell, and repeat for the desired number of repetitions.

Figure 4-48. Power snatch—starting position

Figure 4-49. Power snatch—explosion

Figure 4-50. Power snatch—receiving the barbell

Power Snatches From the Hang

The power snatch can also be performed from the hang. These exercises are easier to learn, but often result in less weight being lifted. The power snatch from the hang has the same variations as the power clean from the hang.

Power Snatch—Hang—Above the Knee

To perform the power snatch from the hang, with the bar above the knee, the athlete will take a snatch-width grip on the bar and stand up with the barbell in his hands. From this point, the athlete will set the back and push the hips back, allowing the barbell to slide down along the thighs until it is just below the level of the hips. This is the starting position (Figure 4-51). From this point, the athlete will perform the explosion as described above and receive the bar overhead. Have the athlete lower and repeat for the desired number of repetitions.

Figure 4-51. Power snatch—hang—above the knee—starting position

Power Snatch—Hang—Knee

To perform the power snatch from the hang, with the bar at the knees, the athlete will assume the same starting position previously described for the power snatch, hang, above the knee variation. From this position, the athlete will continue pushing the hips back and bending the knees until the bar is at knee level. The shoulders should be ahead of the bar in this position. This is the starting position (Figure 4-52). From this point, the athlete will slowly lift the bar past the knees, perform the explosion as described, and receive the bar overhead. Have the athlete lower and repeat for the desired number of repetitions.

Figure 4-52. Power snatch—hang—knee—starting position

Power Snatch—Hang—Below the Knee

To perform the power snatch from the hang, with the bar below the knees, the athlete will assume the starting position described in the power snatch, hang, knees variation described. From there, the athlete will continue pushing the hips back and bending the knees until the bar below knee level. The shoulders should be ahead of the bar in this position. This is the starting position (Figure 4-53). From this point, the athlete will slowly lift the bar around the knees, perform the explosion as described, and receive the bar overhead. Have the athlete lower and repeat for the desired number of repetitions.

Figure 4-53. Power snatch—hang—below the knee—starting position

Snatch Pulls

The snatch pull is a partial movement that has all the benefits of the power snatch, but involves less technique. This exercise can be performed from the floor or from any of the hang positions. This exercise is performed just like the power snatch except that it stops after the explosion (i.e., there is no quarter squat, and the barbell is not lifted overhead).

Jerks

The jerk is an explosive, total-body exercise that involves lifting the bar from shoulder height to a position overhead in one movement. It is a staple of athletic strength and conditioning programs because it is performed standing up, is explosive in nature, and is relatively easy to learn. This chapter will cover two variations of this lift:

- Push jerk
- Split jerk

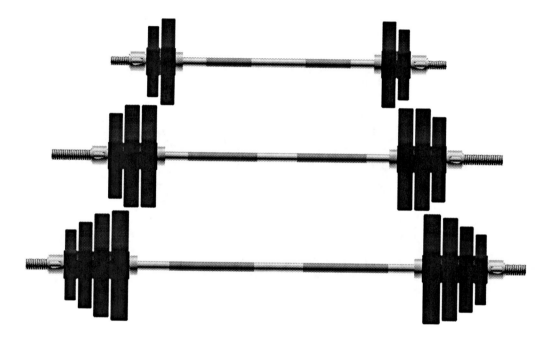

Push Jerk

The push jerk is the simpler of the two variations. This lift begins with the barbell on the front of the shoulders. To perform, the athlete should stand up with the barbell on the front of the shoulder. The bar should be gripped with a shoulder-width grip. The feet should be hip-width apart. The athlete will then set the back. This is the starting position (Figure 4-54). Keeping the weight on the heels, the athlete will quickly descend into a quarter squat (Figure 4-55). Without pausing, the athlete will then explosively extend the knees and hips to drive the bar off the shoulders (Figure 4-56). When the bar reaches eye level, the athlete will press it up and slightly behind the head so that the bar is in line with the hips (Figure 4-57). Have the athlete lower the bar and repeat for the desired number of repetitions.

Figure 4-54. Push jerk—starting position

Figure 4-55. Push jerk—dip

Figure 4-56. Push jerk—drive

Figure 4-57. Push jerk—ending position

Split Jerk

The split jerk requires more technique than the push jerk. For the split jerk, the athlete will assume the same starting position as in the push jerk. Just like with that lift, the athlete will quickly descend into a quarter squat and then reverse directions and drive the barbell off the shoulders. When the bar reaches eye level, the athlete should drop under the bar by moving one foot forward and the other foot backward. The front leg should be bent at the knee, with the front foot flat on the ground. The back leg should have a slight bend at the knee, with the ball of the back foot on the ground. The act of dropping under the bar by moving the feet will force the athlete's body under the bar, allowing the bar to be received on extended arms. The bar should be slightly behind the head and in line with the hips (Figure 4-58). The athlete should recover by moving the front foot back, half the distance, and then move the back foot forward so that it is in line with the front. Have the athlete lower the bar and then repeat for the desired number of repetitions.

Figure 4-58. Split jerk—split position

Cleans, snatches, and jerks can all be performed with a barbell (which is how they are described in this chapter). They can also be performed with dumbbells. Dumbbells require both sides of the body to work independently. When they are done using dumbbells, the fundamental techniques are the exact same, though there may be more variability in terms of how the dumbbells are held and where they are positioned at the end of the movement.

Chapter 5 Kettlebells

Kettlebells are essentially metal balls with a handle. If an exercise can be performed with free weights, it can be done with kettlebells. Having said that, when it comes to the conditioning of athletes, a coach must be concerned with getting the most benefit out of an athlete's limited training time. A great deal more weight can be handled on the free weight exercises than with kettlebells. For most athletes, this makes free weight versions of exercises superior to the kettlebell due to the extra strength, hypertrophy, and power that the athlete must develop with the free weights. Kettlebells do have a number of exercises unique to them that cannot be duplicated by free weights. These exercises potentially provide important benefits. This chapter is going to cover the following exercises:

- Swings
- Cleans
- Snatches
- Jerks
- Get-ups
- Windmills
- Farmer's walk

Swings

Swings are a rhythmic, total-body exercise. They particularly stress the muscles of the lower back, hamstrings, and glutes. Due to their rhythmic nature, this exercise lends itself to being performed for periods of time. This section will cover two variations: the two-handed swing and the one-handed swing.

With both types of swings, two approaches are common. The first is to use a hip hinge to perform the swing. With this approach, the knees are kept soft, but the bulk of the movement is coming from pushing the hips back and then extending them to swing the kettlebell forward. The second is to use a squat to perform the swing. For this approach, the athlete moves into a quarter squat and then extends the hips and knees to swing the kettlebell forward. Both approaches work well; the method used will depend upon whether the coach primarily wants to train the hamstrings and lower back (i.e., hip hinge) or the quadriceps, hamstrings, and glutes (i.e., quarter squat).

Two-Handed Swings

The two-handed swing is the kettlebell exercise that athletes should master first. Because it involves holding a kettlebell with two hands, more weight can be handled than in the one-handed swing. To perform the two-handed swing, begin with the kettlebell on the floor. The athlete should straddle the kettlebell with the feet shoulder-width apart. The athlete should set the back, push the hips back, and squat down to grip the kettlebell. The kettlebell should be gripped with both hands, using an overhand grip. The hands should grip the kettlebell so that they are next to each other. The athlete will stand up, holding the kettlebell in front of the body. Keeping the arms straight, the athlete will push the hips back, allowing the kettlebell to swing backward between the legs (Figure 5-1). The athlete should quickly and smoothly reverse directions, extending the hips and knees. As this happens, the athlete will allow the kettlebell to swing forward until the arms are parallel to the floor (Figure 5-2). With fluid motions, the athlete will repeat the movement for the desired number of repetitions or for the desired amount of time.

Figure 5-1. Two-handed kettlebell swing—starting position

Figure 5-2. Two-handed kettlebell swing—finish

One-Handed Swings

The one-handed swing provides the benefits of the two-handed variation, but allows the athlete to develop each side of the body independently. Due to its one-handed nature, the athlete will be able to handle less weight than in the two-handed version. The setup for this exercise is the same as the two-handed swing. The athlete should grip the kettlebell with the right hand, using an overhand grip. The hand should grip the left corner of the kettlebell's handle. Keeping the arm straight, the athlete should push the hips back, allowing the kettlebell to swing backward between the legs (Figure 5-3). The athlete will quickly and smoothly reverse directions, extending the hips and knees. As this happens, the athlete should allow the kettlebell to swing forward until the arm is parallel to the floor (Figure 5-4). With fluid motions, the athlete should repeat for the desired number of repetitions or for the desired amount of time, and then switch arms.

Figure 5-3. One-handed kettlebell swing—starting position

Figure 5-4. One-handed kettlebell swing—finish

Cleans

The clean is a rhythmic exercise. It is similar to the barbell/dumbbell clean in that the kettlebell ends up on the front of the shoulder. However, it is misnamed in that it is not meant to be a power exercise. This exercise has the same starting position as the one-handed swing, with the kettlebell in the right hand. From this position, the athlete will swing the kettlebell forward by extending the hips and knees. As the kettlebell swings around, the athlete should drop under it in a partial squat, receiving the kettlebell on the front of the right shoulder (Figure 5-5). This process will be repeated for the desired number of repetitions, and then the athlete will switch sides.

Figure 5-5. Kettlebell clean—receiving position

Snatches

Like the clean variation, this is a rhythmic exercise and is somewhat misnamed. This exercise begins in the same position as the kettlebell clean with one important difference: the kettlebell should be gripped toward the middle of the handle. From this position, the kettlebell is swung up. The kettlebell should be received overhead in a partial squat position. As it swings back toward the shoulder, the right arm should drop underneath the kettlebell and should punch up; this motion will help to prevent the kettlebell from slamming against the forearm and causing bruising (Figure 5-6).

Figure 5-6. Kettlebell snatch—receiving position

Jerks

The jerk is also meant to be a rhythmic exercise and should not be programmed as an exercise with a power focus. To perform this exercise, have the athlete stand up with the kettlebell resting on the right shoulder. The right elbow should be elevated with the right hand gripping the handle (palm facing up). The athlete's feet should be hip-width apart, and the back should be set (Figure 5-7). From this position, the athlete will quickly move into a quarter squat and use the legs to drive the kettlebell off the shoulder. As the kettlebell reaches eye level, the athlete should drop under the kettlebell into a quarter squat, receiving it on an extended arm (Figure 5-8). This process will be repeated for the desired number of repetitions, and then the athlete should switch sides.

Figure 5-7. Kettlebell jerk—starting position

Figure 5-8. Kettlebell jerk—receiving position

Get-Ups

The get-up exercise develops balance, coordination, and the athlete's shoulder strength. It is an exercise that has a role in warm-ups, mobility work, and can be used to help strengthen the shoulders to prevent injuries. The athlete begins this exercise by lying down with the kettlebell next to the right shoulder (Figure 5-9). The kettlebell is gripped with the right hand and pressed until the arm is fully extended, with the kettlebell level with the chest. The athlete then bends the right knee, sliding the right foot toward the hips (Figure 5-10). Keeping the right arm extended, the athlete will push off the right foot and roll over onto the left side of the body, using the left arm as support. The athlete will then extend the left arm (Figure 5-11). Keeping the right arm extended, the athlete should push off the left arm and get the legs under the body. After this, the athlete should stand up with the kettlebell held overhead. The athlete will reverse the steps to lie back down and repeat for the desired number of repetitions before switching sides.

Figure 5-9. Get-ups—start

Figure 5-10. Get-ups—preparing to turn

Figure 5-11. Get-ups—preparing to get off the ground

Windmills

Windmills are another kettlebell exercise that develops balance, proprioception, and can be used to help with the athlete's shoulder strength. This exercise can have a role in warm-ups, mobility work, and can be used to help strengthen the shoulders to prevent injuries. To perform windmills, have the athlete stand up with the feet hip-width apart. The athlete should set the back. The kettlebell should be gripped in the right hand and placed on the right shoulder. The athlete will press it up until the arm is fully extended. Next, the athlete should pivot the feet to the left approximately 45 degrees (Figure 5-12). Keeping the right arm extended, the athlete will lean toward the left, allowing the left hand to slide down the left leg as far as is comfortable (Figure 5-13). Have the athlete reverse directions and repeat for the desired number of repetitions before switching.

Figure 5-12. Windmills—start

Figure 5-13. Windmills—descent

Farmer's Walk

The farmer's walk is a classic strongman exercise that develops grip strength and the athlete's core. To perform this exercise, the athlete will need two kettlebells. The exercise begins with the athlete standing up and gripping a kettlebell in each hand. The athlete should set the back, keep the arms straight, and keep the kettlebells close to the body. From this position, while holding the kettlebells, the athlete will walk a specified distance without setting down the kettlebells.

It is important for an athlete to have a chance to learn how to perform these kettlebell exercises before using a great deal of weight with them. Just like any other exercise, too much weight done too soon can result in injuries to the athlete. If there is an interest in using kettlebells as part of an athlete's strength and conditioning program, Figure 5-14 provides an example of a familiarization program that can be used to master techniques and develop endurance for the exercises. Note that this program is meant to be done circuit-style; have the athlete repeat the circuit as many times as desired. This program could be done as part of the athlete's warm-up.

Exercise	Number of Repetitions
Two-handed swings	10
One-handed swings (right hand)	5
One-handed swings (left hand)	5
Cleans (right hand)	5
Cleans (left hand)	5
Snatches (right hand)	5
Snatches (left hand)	5
Jerks (right hand)	5
Jerks (left hand)	5
Get-ups (right hand)	5
Get-ups (left hand)	5
Windmills (right hand)	5
Windmills (left hand)	5

Figure 5-14. Sample kettlebell familiarization program

Chapter 6 Suspension Training

Suspension training involves performing exercises using equipment that is essentially a pair of handles attached to straps that are suspended from an object. These tools are effective for conditioning the untrained. For trained athletes, these tools are useful for metabolic conditioning, endurance training, and developing balance and stability. Suspension training exercises in this chapter will focus on exercises for the following areas:

- Upper back
- Chest
- Shoulders
- Arms
- Core
- Lower body

Upper Back

For the muscles of the upper back, suspension training involves variations of the straight-arm row, inverted row, and pull-ups. All of these exercises are effective at targeting the lats, scapular muscles, deltoids, and biceps. This section will cover the following:

- Straight-arm rows
- Rows
- Pull-ups

Straight-Arm Rows

Straight-arm rows are an exercise that mimics a cable exercise. This exercise targets the lats, shoulders, and even the shoulder extension role of the triceps. To perform this exercise, the straps should be adjusted so that they are hanging at waist height. Have the athlete grip the straps and raise the arms until they are parallel to the ground. The athlete should step back until the straps are under tension. While leaning back, make sure that the athlete keeps a straight line from the ankles through the shoulders (Figure 6-1). Keeping the arms straight, the athlete will push them down toward the floor. As the arms are pushed down, the athlete should allow this motion to lift the body up onto the heels (Figure 6-2). Have the athlete lower under control and repeat.

Figure 6-1. Straight arm rows—starting position

Figure 6-2. Straight arm rows—ending position

Rows

Just like with barbell or dumbbell rows, rows on the suspension trainer develop the muscles of the upper back, shoulder, and biceps. Unlike the barbell and dumbbell, these are not strenuous to the lower back, so they represent a way to maintain fitness during times of injury. The straps should be adjusted so that they are hanging at waist height. The athlete should face the straps, grip them, raise the arms up until they are parallel to the ground, and then step back until the straps are under tension. Next, the athlete will lean back, keeping a straight line from the ankles through the shoulders (Figure 6-3). From this position, the body is pulled toward the handles by flexing the elbows. Note that the elbows should remain at the sides while pulling (Figure 6-4). The athlete should lower and repeat for the desired number of repetitions. While pulling, the athlete should concentrate on pulling the shoulder blades together. While lowering, the focus should be on letting the shoulder blades move apart.

Figure 6-3. Rows—starting position

Figure 6-4. Rows—ending position

To make this exercise more challenging, it can be done by moving the feet forward so that the upper body is closer to the floor (Figure 6-5), while lifting one foot off the ground (Figure 6-6), or using one arm at a time (Figure 6-7).

Figure 6-5. Rows—stepping forward

Figure 6-6. One-legged rows

Figure 6-7. One-arm rows

Pull-Ups

Pull-ups with the suspension trainer develop the muscles of the upper back, shoulder, and biceps. This exercise teaches the athlete to handle his own bodyweight. The unique nature of doing this exercise with the suspension trainer enhances the athlete's proprioception as well as develops the muscles differently because the trainer will move the athlete while they are performing the pull-up. For this exercise, the straps should be adjusted so that they are hanging as high off the ground as possible. Have the athlete grip the straps, lift the feet off the ground, cross the ankles, and allow the arms to fully straighten. From this position, the athlete will flex the elbows and pull the body up as far as possible. While pulling the body up, the athlete should concentrate on moving the shoulder blades together.

Chest

Suspension training is a way to train the muscles of the chest. It allows for a combination of traditional bodyweight exercises (such as push-ups) as well as the performance of exercises that are traditionally free weight exercises (like flies and presses). Like those exercises, it develops several muscle groups together—chest, shoulders, and triceps. This section will cover the following:

- Chest press
- Push-ups
- Flies
- Dips

Chest Press

The chest press develops the muscles of the chest, shoulders, and triceps. This exercise can be thought of as a standing push-up. To perform the chest press, the straps should be adjusted so that they are hanging at waist height. Have the athlete grip each strap and lift the arms until they are parallel to the floor. Next, the athlete will step back, leaning into the straps while keeping the arms straight. The heels, hips, and shoulders should be in line (Figure 6-8). From this position, the athlete will flex the arms and lower the body toward the handles (Figure 6-9). Have the athlete reverse directions and repeat for the desired number of repetitions.

Figure 6-8. Chest press—starting position

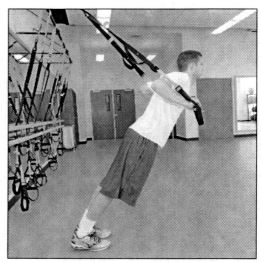
Figure 6-9. Chest press—ending position

To make this exercise more difficult, the straps can be adjusted so that they are hanging closer to the ground. This modification will require the athlete to step farther back to perform the chest press, which requires the body to be closer to the ground.

Push-Ups

Just like push-ups performed on the floor, this exercise develops the chest, shoulders, and triceps. The difference is that this exercise has a balance component due to the unstable nature of the straps, which requires the athlete to use additional muscles. For this exercise, the straps should be adjusted so that they are hanging close to the ground. The athlete will assume the push-up position, placing one hand in each strap (Figure 6-10). From that position, the athlete should lower the body as far down as is comfortable (Figure 6-11). Next, the athlete will reverse directions and repeat for the desired number of repetitions. This exercise can be made more challenging by being performed with one foot lifted off the ground.

Figure 6-10. Push-ups—starting position

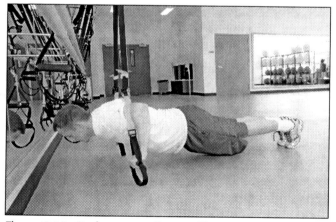

Figure 6-11. Push-ups—ending position

Flies

Much like the free weight version, suspension flies develop the muscles of the chest. Unlike free weights, a balance component will require the recruitment of additional muscles—especially as the athlete advances and performs the exercise closer to the floor. For flies, the straps should be hanging at waist height. The athlete should grip each strap and raise the arms until they are parallel to the floor. The palms should face each other. The athlete will step back, leaning into the straps, while keeping the arms straight. The heels, hips, and shoulders should be in line (Figure 6-12). From this position, the athlete should flex the elbows slightly and spread both hands apart, allowing the body to lean forward as the hands are spread farther apart. This movement should be continued until both hands are even with the body (Figure 6-13). The athlete will then reverse directions and repeat for the desired number of repetitions.

Figure 6-12. Flies—starting position

Figure 6-13. Flies—ending position

Dips

Like the traditional bodyweight version, this exercise develops the muscles of the chest, shoulders, and triceps. The suspension variation is much more challenging than the traditional version and should be considered to be an extremely advanced exercise. The straps should be at waist height or higher. To perform this exercise, the athlete will stand up and grip each strap. Keeping the arms straight, the athlete should pick the feet up off the ground. From this position, the athlete will flex the elbows, lowering the upper body until the upper arms are at least parallel to the floor. The athlete will then reverse direction and repeat. While performing the dips, the athlete should focus on keeping the arms tight to the side of the body.

Shoulders

The shoulders are heavily taxed in the chest and upper back exercises with suspension training. Not only will these muscles flex or extend the shoulder joint, but they will also be involved in stabilizing the body during these exercises. In addition to chest and upper back exercises, other exercises can be performed to stress the muscles of the shoulder when using the suspension trainer. These include the following exercises:

- Reverse flies
- Prone arm raises
- Side raises

Reverse Flies

Reverse flies are an exercise primarily for the rear deltoid muscles. For this exercise, the straps should be adjusted until they are between waist and shoulder height. Have the athlete face the straps, grip them, and then raise the arms up until they are parallel to the ground. The athlete should step back until the straps are under tension and lean back, keeping a straight line from the ankles through the shoulders. From this position, keeping a slight bend at the elbows, the athlete will spread the hands apart and allow the body to rise until the hands are even with the body (Figure 6-14). Have the athlete reverse directions and repeat for the desired number of repetitions.

Figure 6-14. Reverse flies

Prone Arm Raises

Prone arm raises are a challenging exercise that will heavily tax the abdominal/lower back muscles, the shoulders of the exercising arm, and the shoulder of the stabilizing arm. For prone arm raises, the straps should be hanging near the floor. The athlete will assume the push-up position with the feet in the straps (Figure 6-15). Keeping the elbow extended, the athlete should raise the right arm off the ground (Figure 6-16). The athlete will then lower the arm and switch sides.

Figure 6-15. Prone arm raises—starting position

Figure 6-16. Prone arm raises—ending position

Side Raises

Side raises are an advanced exercise primarily targeting the medial deltoids. The straps should be between waist and shoulder height. For this exercise, pull one strap through the other. The athlete will position the body so that the right side is facing the strap. The athlete should grip the strap with the right hand. While this step is being done, the athlete will extend the right arm and lean toward the left. The athlete should move the feet so that they are beneath the strap while keeping a straight line from the heels through the shoulders (Figure 6-17). Keeping the right arm straight, the athlete will use the deltoids to bring the right hand down toward the body, allowing the body to move toward the strap at the same time (Figure 6-18). The athlete should then relax, allowing the hand to move back up, and repeat for the desired number of repetitions.

Figure 6-17. Side raises—starting position

Figure 6-18. Side raises—ending position

Arms

The chest, upper back, and shoulder exercises described to this point all stress the biceps and triceps to an extent. Even with suspension training, these muscles are still involved in flexing the elbow, extending the elbow, and maintaining the various positions. The following exercises can be performed with suspension trainers to specifically target the biceps and triceps:

- Biceps curls
- Triceps extensions

Biceps Curls

This exercise is meant to focus on the biceps. To perform it, the straps should be adjusted so that they are hanging between waist and shoulder height. The athlete should grip the straps and lift the arms up until they are parallel to the ground. Next, have the athlete step back until the straps are under tension. The athlete's hands should be supinated. The athlete will lean back, keeping a straight line from the ankles through the shoulders (Figure 6-19). From this position, keeping the upper arms locked in place, the athlete should pull the body toward the handles using the biceps (Figure 6-20). The athlete should lower and repeat for the desired number of repetitions.

Figure 6-19. Biceps curls—starting position

Figure 6-20. Biceps curls—ending position

Triceps Extensions

Triceps extensions are an isolation exercise targeting the triceps. For triceps extensions, the straps will be adjusted so that they are hanging at waist height. The athlete should grip each strap and lift the arms until they are parallel to the floor. The athlete should step back, leaning into the straps. The arms should be straight. The athlete should rotate the arms so that the elbows point toward the floor with the heels, hips, and shoulders in line (Figure 6-21). From this position, keeping the upper arms locked in place, the athlete should flex the elbows and lower the head toward the handles (Figure 6-22). Have the athlete reverse directions and repeat for the desired number of repetitions.

Figure 6-21. Triceps extensions—starting position

Figure 6-22. Triceps extensions—ending position

Core

The muscles of the abdomen and lower back are stressed in most of the suspension trainer exercises that have been described up to this point. In the majority of these exercises, those muscles have a stabilizing role and are essential to maintaining both good posture and balance. The following exercises can be performed using the suspension trainer to directly stress these muscles:

- Prone knees to chest
- Prone V-ups
- Supine hips up
- Supine hips back
- Supine clocks
- Supine leg raises
- Standing rotations

Prone Knees to Chest

In addition to focusing on the muscles of the core, this exercise also develops upper body endurance. The straps should be adjusted so that they are hanging close to the ground. To perform this exercise, the athlete will assume the push-up position with the feet in the straps. From this position, keeping the hands in place, the athlete will bring the knees up toward the stomach (Figure 6-23).

Figure 6-23. Prone knees to chest—ending position

Prone V-Ups

Prone V-ups are an advanced version of the prone knees exercise. This exercise has the same starting position as the prone knee to chest exercise. From the starting position, keeping the hands in place, the athlete will lift the hips as high into the air as possible. As the hips are being lifted, the legs and arms should remain straight (Figure 6-24).

Figure 6-24. Prone V-ups—ending position

Supine Hips Up

Unlike the previous two exercises, this exercise does not require upper body endurance. To perform this exercise, the straps should be adjusted so that they at between knee-height and waist-height. The athlete should lie down on the ground so that the eyes are under the straps. The athlete will reach up and grip the straps. Keeping the legs straight, the athlete should lift them off the ground until they make a 90-degree angle with the ground. Holding onto the straps, the athlete will lift the hips straight up off the ground (Figure 6-25).

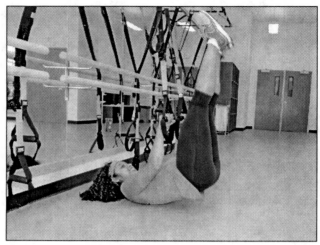

Figure 6-25. Supine hips up—ending position

Supine Hips Back

Supine hips back is another core exercise that will also develop some upper body endurance. To perform this exercise, the straps should be adjusted so that they are hanging close to the ground. The athlete will sit in front of the straps, facing them. Next, the athlete will extend the legs in front of the body and place the feet in the straps. The athlete will place the hands next to the hips and extend the arms so that the arms are supporting the body's weight (Figure 6-26). Keeping the arms straight, the athlete will push the hips forward and then pull the hips back toward the starting position (Figure 6-27).

Figure 6-26. Supine hips back—starting position

Figure 6-27. Supine hips back—ending position

Supine Clocks

Like with supine hips up, this exercise does not require upper body endurance. The athlete will assume the same starting position described in the supine hips up exercise. Holding onto the straps, the athlete will turn the hips and lower the legs to the left side of the body (Figure 6-28). The athlete will then raise the legs and lower them to the other side. Have the athlete repeat for the desired number of repetitions.

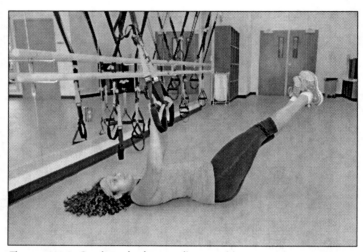

Figure 6-28. Supine clocks—ending position

Supine Leg Raises

Supine leg raises are another exercise performed lying down. To perform this exercise, the athlete will assume the same starting position described in the supine clocks. Keeping the legs together and straight, the athlete will lift them off the ground approximately 12 inches and then lower and repeat for the desired number of repetitions.

Standing Rotations

Standing rotations are an advanced exercise. The straps should be adjusted so that they are between waist-height and shoulder-height. One strap will be pulled through the other. The athlete will stand so that the feet are under the strap. The athlete will grip the strap with both hands and, while keeping a straight line from the heels to the shoulder, will lean back until the arms are straight (Figure 6-29). Keeping the arms straight, the athlete will turn the hips and shoulders to the left side (Figure 6-30). The athlete will then turn back to the starting position. Next, have the athlete repeat to the right side.

Figure 6-29. Standing rotations—starting position

Figure 6-30. Standing rotations—ending position

Lower Body

Suspension training lends itself to a number of exercises that target the lower body. These exercises include the following:

- Squats
- One-legged squats
- Reverse lunges
- Hip lifts
- Lying leg curls

Squats

Squats involve the glutes, quadriceps, hamstrings, and calves. For this exercise, the straps should be adjusted so that they are between waist-height and shoulder-height. The athlete will grip the straps and step back until the arms are straight. Their feet should be hip-width apart, and the back should be set (Figure 6-31). Holding onto the straps, the athlete will squat down by pushing the hips back. While squatting, make sure that the athlete keeps the feet flat and the weight on the heels (Figure 6-32). Next, the athlete will reverse directions and repeat for the desired number of repetitions.

Figure 6-31. Squats—starting position

Figure 6-32. Squats—ending position

One-Legged Squats

One-legged squats require more balance than the two-legged version. They may also have more sports-specificity in sports that require the athlete to lever off one side of the body. They have the same starting position as squats. Holding onto the straps, the athlete will lift the right foot off the ground (Figure 6-33). Holding the right foot up, the athlete will push the hips back and squat down using the left leg. While squatting, the athlete should keep the foot flat and the weight on the heel (Figure 6-34). The athlete will reverse directions and repeat for the desired number of repetitions before switching legs.

Figure 6-33. One-legged squats—starting position

Figure 6-34. One-legged squats—ending position

Reverse Lunges

Reverse lunges develop the glutes, hamstrings, and quadriceps. They also require balance to perform. They have the same starting position as the previous two exercises. Holding onto the straps, the athlete will lift the right knee until the right thigh is parallel to the floor. From this position, have the athlete take a big step back with the right leg. As the right foot moves back, the athlete will lower the body using the left leg until the left thigh is parallel to the floor (Figure 6-35). The athlete should reverse directions and repeat for the desired number of repetitions before switching legs.

Figure 6-35. Reverse lunges—ending position

Hip Lifts

Hip lifts are a hamstring exercise. This exercise is also commonly performed on the stability ball. To perform it using the suspension trainer, the straps should be adjusted so that they are at knee height. The athlete will lie down facing up and place the feet in the straps. The legs should be straight (Figure 6-36). Keeping the legs straight, the athlete will lift the hips off the ground as high as possible (Figure 6-37). Next, the athlete will lower and repeat for the desired number of repetitions.

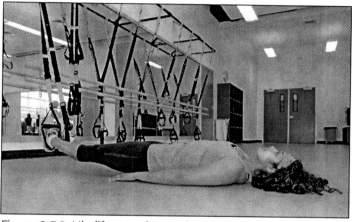

Figure 6-36. Hip lifts—starting position

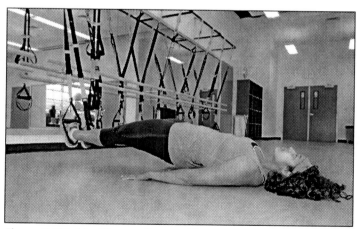

Figure 6-37. Hip lifts—ending position

Lying Leg Curls

Lying leg curls are another hamstring exercise. It is an advanced version of the hip lift and has the same starting position. From the starting position, the athlete will keep the legs straight and lift the hips off the ground as high as is comfortable. From this position, the athlete will curl the heels toward the hips (Figure 6-38). The athlete will then extend the legs with the hips up. Have the athlete repeat for the desired number of repetitions.

Figure 6-38. Lying leg curls—ending position

If an athlete is unfamiliar with suspension training, then some time should be spent familiarizing him with it prior to incorporating it in the workout proper. Until the athlete is familiar with a tool, performance will be limited by the skill in performing the exercise, which is going to severely limit the ability of the coach to program. Figures 6-39 and 6-40 provide examples of two programs that can be used as part of athletes' warm-up to help familiarize them with suspension training. Note that each program is meant to be done circuit-style, with each exercise being performed for a specified time. There should be little to no rest between exercises. Have athletes repeat the circuit as many times as needed.

Exercise	Time (in seconds)
Squats	30
Hip lifts	30
Chest press	30
Flies	30
Rows	30
Pull-ups	30
Reverse flies	30
Biceps curls	30
Triceps extensions	30
Prone knees to chest	30
Supine leg raises	30

Figure 6-39. Sample suspension training circuit

Exercise	Time (in seconds)
One-legged squats	30
Reverse lunges	30
Lying leg curls	30
Chest press—one foot	30
Push-ups	30
Straight-arm rows	30
Pull-ups	30
Reverse flies	30
Prone arm raises	30
Biceps curls	30
Triceps extensions	30
Prone V-ups	30
Supine clocks	30

Figure 6-40. Sample advanced suspension training circuit

Chapter 7 Heavy Ropes

Heavy ropes use long, extra-thick rope that is generally anchored to something in order to allow the exercises to be performed. These total-body exercises are effective strength and conditioning tools for the untrained. For athletes, these exercises are excellent warm-up exercises and can help with metabolic conditioning. This chapter will cover the following categories of exercises:

- Slams
- Circles
- Chops
- Twists

Slams

Slams involve using the entire body to lift up and then slam down the heavy ropes. This motion involves exerting force against the ground and flexing and extending the trunk and shoulders. This means that just about every muscle in the body is involved in performing slams. Slams have several variations:

- Two-handed slams
- One-handed slams
- One-legged slams
- Lunge slams
- Shuffle slams
- Backpedal slams

Two-Handed Slams

Two-handed slams are performed by simultaneously slamming an end of the rope being held in each hand against the ground. To perform, have the athlete stand up, place the feet hip-width apart, and set the back. The athlete should grab an end of the heavy rope in each hand and then lift both arms until they are parallel to the ground (Figure 7-1). Keeping the weight on the heels, the athlete will push the hips back and move into a quarter squat. As this step is being done, the athlete should keep the arms straight and slam the rope against the ground (Figure 7-2). Without pausing, the athlete will stand up quickly out of the squat and lift the arms back up to parallel. The athlete should repeat for the desired number of repetitions or the desired amount of time, making this motion rhythmic.

Figure 7-1. Two-handed slams—starting position

Figure 7-2. Two-handed slams—the slam

One-Handed Slams

The one-handed slam requires more coordination from the athlete to successfully perform the exercise. This exercise begins in the same way as the two-handed slam. The difference is that only one hand slams the rope to the ground at a time (Figure 7-3). After slamming, the athlete will stand up quickly out of the squat and lift the other arm up to parallel. Next, the athlete will quickly squat down while slamming the rope in the other hand against the ground. The athlete should make sure to alternate between the right and left sides.

Figure 7-3. One-handed slams—right-handed slam

One-Legged Slams

Performing slams while standing on one leg requires the athlete to develop balance and also helps to develop the ankle joint, making this a great exercise for advanced rehab or for ankle prehab. This exercise begins just like the previous two. After lifting the rope, the athlete will lift the right foot off the ground (Figure 7-4). Keeping the weight on the left heel, the athlete will push the hips back and move into a quarter squat. As this step is being done, the athlete will keep the arms straight and slam the rope against the ground. Without pausing, the athlete will stand up quickly out of the squat and lift the arms back up to parallel. After the desired number of repetitions have been performed, the athlete will switch legs. To make the one-legged slam more advanced, the exercise can also be performed on an unstable surface.

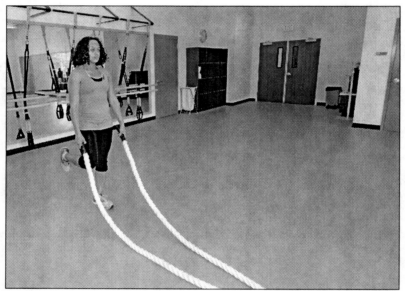

Figure 7-4. One-legged slam

Lunge Slams

Performing the slam in conjunction with a lunge enhances balance, coordination, and mobility. This exercise begins just like the previous slams. From the starting position, the athlete will take a big step back with the left foot. As the left foot steps back, the athlete will flex the right hip and knee until the right thigh is parallel to the floor. As this is being done, the athlete should keep the arms straight and slam the rope against the ground (Figure 7-5). Without pausing, the athlete will stand up quickly out of the lunge and lift the arms back up to parallel. The athlete will then step back with the right foot and repeat the exercise. Have the athlete continue alternating feet for the desired number of repetitions or the desired time, making this a rhythmic motion.

Figure 7-5. Lunge slam

Shuffle Slams

The shuffle slam adds an athletic movement to the slam exercise and has the same starting position as the previous exercises. From this position, the athlete will push off the right foot and step to the side with the left. As this step is being done, the athlete will keep the arms straight and slam the rope against the ground. While slamming the rope, have the athlete bring the right foot back so that the feet are hip-width apart. Have the athlete repeat for the desired distance and then shuffle in the opposite direction.

Backpedal Slams

The backpedal is another athletic movement that can be added to make the slam exercise more challenging. It also begins from the same starting position as the previous slams. Standing close to the middle of the full length of the rope, the athlete will maintain a low center of gravity and move backward by picking up the feet and stepping back. As this step is being done, the athlete will keep the arms straight and slam the rope against the ground. Have the athlete repeat for the desired distance.

Circles

Circles are an exercise performed out of the athletic ready position, but their primary focus is on the upper body. With this exercise, the lower body and trunk will stabilize the athlete while the muscles that act on the shoulder and arm will be performing the exercise. To perform circles, the athlete will get into the same starting position as the slams that were described previously. He will lift both arms until they are parallel to the ground. From this position, the arms will make large clockwise circles. After the desired number of repetitions, the athlete should reverse directions and make large counterclockwise circles with the arms. Circles can also be combined with other movements like backpedals, shuffles, lunges, squats, and the like.

Chops

Chops are meant to be a total-body exercise. With chops, the ropes are lifted overhead and then forced toward the ground in a motion similar to striking firewood with an axe. Not only does this exercise train the muscles of the upper body and the lower body, but the abdominal and lower back muscles are involved as well. The major variations are:
  • Overhead chop
  • Woodchopper

Overhead Chop

The overhead chop involves lifting the rope overhead and then forcing it straight down. To perform this chop, the athlete should get into a similar starting position as the previous exercises. Once the rope has been picked up, the athlete will hold both hands together and lift both arms until they are overhead (Figure 7-6). From this position, the trunk will be flexed while chopping downward with both arms (Figure 7-7).

Figure 7-6. Overhead chop—start

Figure 7-7. Overhead chop—finish

Woodchoppers

Woodchoppers are performed to an angle, rather than just straight up and down. The athlete will get into the same starting position as the overhead chop. The athlete should lift both arms until they are above the right shoulder (Figure 7-8). From this position, the athlete will flex the trunk while chopping downward with both arms toward the left knee (Figure 7-9). After performing the desired number of repetitions, the athlete will switch sides.

Figure 7-8. Woodchopper—start

Figure 7-9. Woodchopper—finish

Chops can also be done by incorporating other movement patterns. For example, standing on one leg, squatting, lunging, shuffling, backpedaling, and even moving forward.

Twists

Twists are an exercise that is performed out of the athletic ready position. For this exercise, the upper body and lower body must stabilize while the abdominal and lower back muscles are performing the work. To perform twists, the athlete will get into the same starting position as the previous exercises. The athlete should grab an end of the heavy rope in each hand and hold both hands together. The athlete will lift both arms until they are parallel to the floor (Figure 7-10). Keeping the arms parallel to the floor, the athlete will turn quickly to the right (Figure 7-11). Without pausing, the athlete will reverse directions and turn quickly to the left. While turning, the feet should remain planted on the ground. The athlete should concentrate on turning the upper body and keeping the core tight. Twists can also be done by standing on one leg or on an unstable surface to increase their difficulty.

Figure 7-10. Twists—starting position

Figure 7-11. Twists—twisting to the right

Heavy ropes require skill to perform the exercises. The following is a sample routine that an athlete can do to help become oriented to the ropes. This routine should be performed circuit-style without resting in between the exercises. Figure 7-12 lists the exercises as well as the time (in seconds) that each exercise should be performed.

Exercise	Time (in seconds)
Two-handed slams	30
Circles	30
Twists	30
One-handed slams	30
Lunge circles	30
Overhead chops	30
Lunge slams	30
Backpedal circles	30
Twists	30
Woodchoppers	30
Shuffle slams	30
Shuffle circles	30

Figure 7-12. Sample workout with the heavy ropes

Chapter 8 Sandbag Training

Except for the unfit, sandbag training is not going to be an optimal tool for increasing strength and power; it's just too difficult to provide enough overload. This tool is useful in situations where other equipment isn't available, it's useful for metabolic conditioning, and it's very good for developing proprioception and for teaching the athlete to excel in environments that aren't ideal. This chapter will cover the following exercises:

- Cleans
- Snatches
- High pulls
- Squats
- Lunges
- Deadlifts

Cleans

This exercise has more similarities with the kettlebell variation than the barbell in the sense that it is a rhythmic exercise rather than explosive. Due to their bulk, sandbags do not lend themselves to resting on the front of an athlete's shoulders. Because of this, the techniques for the clean exercise must be altered. Even so, this can still be an effective total-body exercise. This section will cover two variations of the clean exercise:

- Cleans
- Split cleans

Cleans

This exercise begins with the sandbag on the floor. The athlete should straddle the sandbag. The athlete should set the back. The arms should be straight and reaching down toward the ground. Keeping the weight on the heels, the athlete will squat down and grip the sandbag (Figure 8-1). From this position, the athlete should extend the hips, knees, and shoulders. Once the sandbag reaches mid-thigh level, the athlete will explosively extend the hips, allowing the sandbag to swing up. As it reaches shoulder level, the athlete will release the grip on the sandbag and extend the arms under the bag, catching it in the crook of the elbows (Figure 8-2). The athlete should then stand up with the bag in the crook of the elbows.

Figure 8-1. Sandbag clean—starting position

Figure 8-2. Sandbag clean—receiving position

Split Cleans

This exercise begins in the same manner as the clean. As the sandbag reaches mid-thigh level, the athlete will explosively extend the hips allowing the sandbag to swing up. As the sandbag reaches shoulder height, the athlete will push one foot forward and one backward. The front foot should land flat on the ground, with the hip and knee flexed. The rear foot should land with the balls of the foot in contact with the ground and a slight bend in the knee. As this happens, the athlete will release the grip on the sandbag and extend the arms under the bag (Figure 8-3), catching it in the crook of the elbows.

Figure 8-3. Sandbag split clean—receiving position

Snatches

In a sense, this snatch exercise is misnamed, as it is not a true snatch. It is more of a swing that is received overhead, just like with the kettlebell version. This exercise begins the same as both the clean exercises already described. As the sandbag reaches mid-thigh level, the athlete will violently extend the hips and allow the bag to swing up. The bag will swing up all the way and be received on straight arms overhead (Figure 8-4).

Figure 8-4. Sandbag snatch—receiving position

High Pulls

The high pull exercise begins the same as the clean and snatch exercises already described. As the sandbag reaches mid-thigh level, the athlete will violently extend the hips and allow the bag to swing up. As the bag reaches abdominal level, the athlete will relax the arms and allow the bag to be accelerated to the height of the shoulders (Figure 8-5).

Figure 8-5. Sandbag high pulls—ending position

Squats

Sandbags allow for squats to be performed to develop the muscles of the lower extremity. The two types of squats that this section will cover are:
- Back squats
- Zercher squats

Back Squats

Back squats begin with the sandbag being held on the back of the athlete's shoulders. The athlete's feet should be hip-width apart, and the back should be set (Figure 8-6). From this position, the athlete will squat down by pushing the hips back and flexing the knees. The athlete should squat down as far as is desired, and then reverse directions.

Figure 8-6. Sandbag back squats—beginning position

Zercher Squats

Given the unusual size and shape of the sandbag, Zercher squats are actually an easier variation for athletes to perform than the back squat described previously. To perform this exercise, the athlete should perform the sandbag clean so that the bag is resting in the crooks of the elbows. From this position, the athlete will place the feet hip-width apart and set the back. Holding the sandbag, the athlete will squat down by pushing the hips back and flexing the knees. The athlete should squat down as far as is comfortable (Figure 8-7).

Figure 8-7. Zercher sandbag squats—ending position

Lunges

The unique nature of sandbags, with the weight shifting around as the athlete moves, serves to make lunges extremely challenging. The sandbags allow for the athlete to develop better balance and proprioception. This section will cover the following types of lunges:

- Zercher lunges
- Overhead lunges
- Rotational reverse lunges

Zercher Lunges

The Zercher lunge begins by cleaning the sandbag as has been described in the sandbag clean exercise at the beginning of this chapter. Once the bag is in the crook of the elbows, the athlete will stand up straight and set the back. From this point, the athlete will take a large step forward with the left foot. The foot should strike the ground in a heel-to-toe manner. As the foot strikes the ground, the athlete should flex the front knee and hip. The athlete will lower the body until the back knee is almost touching the ground (Figure 8-8). The athlete should recover by taking as many steps backward as is necessary to return to the starting position and get the feet in line. The athlete will then repeat with the opposite leg.

Figure 8-8. Zercher sandbag lunge—bottom position

Overhead Lunges

To perform the overhead lunge, the athlete should snatch the sandbag overhead as was described earlier in this chapter. The athlete should try to keep the sandbag positioned slightly behind the head on locked-out arms. From this position, the athlete will take a large step forward with the left foot. The athlete should step forward in a heel-to-toe manner. As the foot strikes the ground, the athlete will flex the left hip and knee to lower the body. The athlete should lower the body until the back knee almost touches the ground, and then take as many steps as necessary to return to the starting position (Figure 8-9). Next, the athlete should switch legs.

Figure 8-9. Overhead sandbag lunge—bottom position

Rotational Reverse Lunges

The rotational reverse lunge begins with the sandbag on the ground. The athlete will squat down, grip it, and stand up with the sandbag (Figure 8-10). From this position, the athlete will set the back. This lunge is performed by taking a large step backward with the left foot. As this step is done, several things should happen. First, the athlete's right knee and hip should be flexed, which will lower the body. The body should be lowered until the back knee is almost touching the ground. As the body is lowered, the upper body and the sandbag should be twisted to the athlete's right (Figure 8-11). From this position, the back leg should step forward while the sandbag is brought back to its original position in front of the body. The athlete will step back with the right leg, rotating the bag toward the left side.

Figure 8-10. Sandbag rotational reverse lunge—starting position

Figure 8-11. Sandbag rotational reverse lunge—bottom position

Deadlifts

Sandbags don't allow for the same amount of weight to be handled in deadlift exercises as barbells. However, the nature of the sandbag makes this an easier exercise to perform for individuals with injuries. Sandbags also allow for rotational movements to be added to the deadlift. This section will cover deadlifts and rotational deadlifts.

Deadlifts

To perform the sandbag deadlift, the athlete will straddle the sandbag. From this position, the athlete will set the back and squat down until the sandbag can be gripped with straight arms (Figure 8-12). From this position, the athlete should extend the knees and hips until standing straight up with the bag (Figure 8-13).

Figure 8-12. Sandbag deadlift—starting position

Figure 8-13. Sandbag deadlift—ending position

Rotational Deadlifts

This exercise begins just like the sandbag deadlift described previously. As the bag is being lifted off the ground, the athlete will twist the upper body and the bag to the right (Figure 8-14). Then, the athlete will lower the bag and on the next repetition twist the bag to the left.

Figure 8-14. Sandbag rotational deadlift—ending position

Figure 8-15 provides a circuit-style workout that can help familiarize athletes with the techniques involved in some of the sandbag exercises described in this chapter. This workout can be used as part of the athlete's warm-up. With this workout, each exercise should be performed for 30 seconds. There should be no rest between the exercises. The athlete will repeat the circuit three times.

Exercise	Duration (in seconds)
Sandbag snatches	30
Sandbag cleans	30
Sandbag Zercher squats	30
Sandbag Zercher lunges (right leg)	30
Sandbag Zercher lunges (left leg)	30
Sandbag deadlifts	30

Figure 8-15. Sample familiarization workout using sandbags

Chapter 9 Speed, Agility, and Plyometrics

Speed, agility, and plyometric exercises are meant to apply the fitness developed in the weight room to the sport. These exercises harness strength and power and apply them to running faster, jumping higher, throwing farther, or changing directions more quickly. This is done by teaching the athlete how to do these things and then applying those skills and abilities to the athlete's sport-specific movement patterns. This chapter will focus on the following speed, agility, and plyometric exercises:

- Technique drills
- Resisted/assisted sprinting
- Vertical plyometrics
- Horizontal plyometrics
- Throws
- Advanced drills

Technique Drills

Technique drills serve a number of important functions. First, they break a complicated motor skill down into its components, making it easier to learn. Second, they can serve as remedial work if an athlete is experiencing a flaw in their technique. Finally, they provide an excellent warm-up once an athlete has mastered the entire movement.

While they have benefits, technique drills need to be kept in perspective. They are not a substitute for performing the entire movement. For example, speed technique drills teach the parts of the sprinting motion, but an athlete still needs to practice sprinting to become better at running fast. Technique drills also need to be performed with good technique, otherwise they reinforce bad habits that can have a negative impact on performance.

This section will cover two broad categories of technique drills:
- Speed technique drills
- Agility technique drills

Speed Technique Drills

With speed training, these technique drills are designed to break the sprinting motion down into component parts. These drills typically progress from the ground up. They begin by focusing on how to contact the ground, how to lift the foot up, how to lift the knee, and finally they put everything together. Each of the technique drills covered in this section is normally performed for 10 to 20 yards. This section will cover the following speed technique drills:

- Ankling
- Heel to hip
- High knees
- A drills

Ankling

Ankling teaches how to contact the ground with the foot. These drills begin with the athlete standing up tall and facing the course. Keeping the legs straight, the athlete should shift the center of gravity forward and plantarflex the right ankle (Figure 9-1). As the center of gravity moves forward, the athlete will allow the right foot to break contact with the ground. As this is done, the athlete should "cast" the right foot. Casting the foot refers to dorsiflexing the ankle (Figure 9-2). Keeping the right leg straight and the right ankle cast, the athlete will step forward with the right foot, landing on the ball of the foot (Figure 9-3). Repeat with the left side. The athlete should continue alternating and perform for the desired distance.

Figure 9-1. Ankling—preparing to step forward

Figure 9-2. Ankling—casting the right foot

Figure 9-3. Ankling—landing

Heel to Hip

The heel to hip drill reinforces the movement patterns learned with ankling and teaches the athlete how to lift the foot to the hip, which is also known as backside mechanics. This skill is important because it helps the athlete to swing the leg forward more quickly during sprinting. For this drill, the athlete will face the course. Keeping the legs straight, the athlete should shift the center of gravity forward. As this is done, the athlete will plantarflex the right ankle. The right foot will break contact with the ground and the ankle should be cast. Keeping the right ankle cast, the athlete will slide the foot up to the right hip (Figure 9-4). To perform this drill properly, the athlete should picture sliding the foot up a wall positioned just behind the body. Keeping the ankle cast, the athlete will place the foot on the ground so that the ball of the foot contacts the ground. The athlete performs with the left side, continuing to alternate for the desired distance.

Figure 9-4. Heel to hip—bringing the heel to the hip

High Knees

The high knee drill teaches the athlete how to lift the knee. This action is also known as frontside mechanics. The athlete will begin this drill by facing the course. The athlete will lift the right knee until the thigh is parallel to the ground. As the foot breaks contact with the ground, the ankle should be cast (Figure 9-5). The foot will be placed on the ground in front of the center of gravity by landing on the ball of the foot. This drill alternates legs for the desired distance.

Figure 9-5. High knee drill—lifting the knee

A Drills

The A drill puts everything together. For this drill, the athlete will begin by facing the course. The athlete will shift the center of gravity forward. As this happens, the athlete will plantarflex the right foot. Once the right foot breaks contact with the ground, the athlete will cast the ankle and pull the foot up toward the right hip. As the foot is lifted toward the right hip, the athlete will cycle the foot forward so that the thigh is parallel to the ground. As the foot cycles forward, it will break contact with the hip and swing forward. The athlete should drive the foot down toward the ground so that it lands in front of the hips and contacts the ground using the ball of the foot. The athlete will pull the hips forward using the right leg and perform the drill with the left leg. The athlete continues alternating for the desired distance.

The drills can be performed as described, or they can be simplified or made more complicated. For example, the drills covered can be performed focusing on one leg at a time (for example, perform with the right leg only for 10 yards, and then perform with the left), then progress to alternating legs. They can also be performed at slow speeds or at fast speeds, e.g., each drill can be performed at a walk, then progress into a jog.

Agility Technique Drills

Agility technique drills are intended to teach fundamental movement patterns. These may vary by sport and even by position. When learning these movement patterns, the drills should be performed for 10 to 20 yards. In general, the following fundamental movement patterns can be adapted to different situations:
- Shuffle
- Backpedal
- Turn
- Zigzag

Shuffle

To perform the shuffle, the athlete will stand with the right side of the body facing the course. The feet should be hip-width apart with the weight on the balls of the feet. The hips should be pushed back with the knees slightly flexed. The athlete's hands should be at a level between waist and shoulder height. The head should face forward (Figure 9-6). To shuffle to the right, the athlete will push off the left foot and step with the right. These should be short, quick steps with the feet maintaining the shoulder-width separation. The movement should be reversed to shuffle to the left (i.e., push off the right foot and step with the left).

Figure 9-6. Shuffle—ready position

Backpedal

The backpedal is performed from the same ready position as the shuffle. For this drill, the athlete will face away from the course. When backpedaling, it is important that the athlete keep the hips low and move backward by lifting the entire foot off the ground. Like with forward sprinting, the focus should be on landing on the balls of the feet while taking short, quick steps backward.

Turn

The turn is initially learned as a 90-degree turn. Set up a cone approximately 10 yards from the start line, and have the athlete face the course. The athlete should run toward the cone. Upon reaching the cone, the athlete will turn toward the right. This is done by shortening the steps as the athlete approaches the cone and extending the right arm downward while dropping the right shoulder. This movement allows the turn to be performed tightly, rotating around the right arm (Figure 9-7). To turn to the left, the athlete would extend the left arm and drop the left shoulder during the turn.

Figure 9-7. Turning to the right—note the right arm and shoulder

Zigzag

The zigzag is a cutting movement. A simple drill helps to teach athletes how to perform this movement. Set up four cones as shown in Figure 9-8. Cones 1 and 4 should be 10 yards apart, with cones 2 and 3 set in-between and off-center. The athlete should begin at cone 1 and run to cone 2. Upon approaching cone 2, the athlete will run to the outside of the cone, shift the weight to the right foot, and push off the right foot, stepping with the left foot toward cone 3. Upon reaching cone 3, the athlete will run to the outside of the cone and shift the weight to the left foot and push off the left foot, stepping with the right foot toward cone 4. The athlete will finish by running through cone 4.

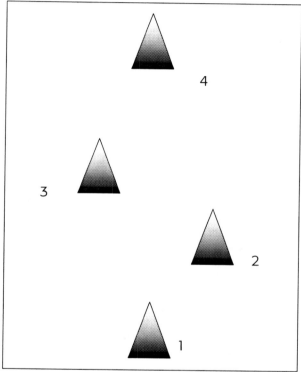

Figure 9-8. Zigzag drill

Resisted/Assisted Sprinting

Resisted and assisted sprinting are both tools that are designed to help teach an athlete how to move the limbs more quickly and how to exert more force against the ground. Both of these tools are effective, but both have limitations as well.

Resisted Sprinting

Resisted sprinting involves making the sprinting motion more difficult by adding some type of weight to the athlete. This additional weight can be in the form of a weighted vest, a parachute, towing a heavy object like a sled or a tire, or even running uphill. The intent is that by making the movement more difficult, the athlete will have to recruit more motor units to perform the movement. Over time, this will become a learned movement pattern, which will allow the athlete to harness these additional motor units during unresisted sprinting, allowing the athlete to sprint faster.

Care should be exercised with this training tool. Too much resistance leads to bad technique, which usually manifests itself by the athlete leaning forward to overcome the resistance (Figure 9-9). When this lean happens, the athlete is unable to extend the hip completely, limiting force application against the ground. This bad habit can become a learned technique, making the tool counterproductive to speed development.

Figure 9-9. Leaning forward during resisted sprinting

With this in mind, guidelines should be followed for resisted sprinting. First, proper running mechanics should be demanded when athletes are using this tool. Second, the resistance should not slow the athlete down by more than 10 percent. Third, when technique or speed suffers, it is time to end the drill. Following these guidelines will keep resistance an effective training tool.

Assisted Sprinting

Assisted sprinting makes the sprinting motion easier, allowing the athlete to run faster than they are normally capable of doing. The idea is that the athlete recruits those additional motor units, learns to move the limbs more quickly, and over time this will translate into faster unassisted performance. The number of ways to accomplish this includes high-speed treadmills, having the athlete towed by something that makes him move quickly, or by running downhill.

This training tool also requires care. Too much speed is just as bad as not enough. When the athlete achieves too much speed on these drills, there is a tendency to lean backward and take strides that are too large. This increased stride limits the force application against the ground and actually causes the athlete to brake as he runs, both of which can become learned running patterns if care is not taken.

To avoid these problems, keep these few guidelines in mind with assisted sprinting. First, proper running mechanics need to be emphasized. Second, the assistance should not allow the athlete to attain speed greater than 106 percent of his maximal speed. Third, when technique or speed suffers, it is time to end the drill.

Vertical Plyometrics

Vertical plyometrics are typically learned using a progression. This progression first focuses on how to explode and how to land safely. Following that, the athlete should learn how to jump onto an object. The last progression involves dropping from a height, reacting to the ground, and exploding. The exercises that involve vertical plyometrics include the following:

- Squat jump
- Countermovement jump
- Box jump
- Depth jump

Squat Jump

The squat jump teaches the basics of the vertical jumping motion as well as how to land safely. To perform this exercise, the athlete will stand with the feet hip-width apart and place the hands behind the head or behind the back. Have the athlete squat down into at least a quarter squat and hold this position for a count. From the squat, the athlete will explode and jump as high as possible. The athlete will land back in the quarter squat, focusing on landing with the hips pushed back so that the glutes and hamstrings absorb the landing (Figure 9-10).

Figure 9-10. Landing during the squat jump

Countermovement Jump

The countermovement jump reinforces landing, but also teaches the athlete how to use a fast squat to generate a higher jump. To perform this exercise, the athlete should stand with the feet hip-width apart. The hands should be at the sides. Pushing the hips back, the athlete should quickly move into a quarter squat. As the squat is being performed, the athlete will swing the arms back. Without pausing in the squat, the athlete should explode upward while swinging the arms up. When leaving the ground, the athlete will reach as high as possible. The athlete should land back in the quarter squat, with the glutes and hamstrings absorbing the landing.

Box Jump

Box jumps teach the athlete how to jump onto a box. It's important to place the boxes on non-slip surfaces, so the boxes don't move while the athlete is jumping onto or off of them. Jumping onto the box helps to enhance vertical power by providing greater heights for the athlete to attempt to jump.

To perform drills that involve jumping on the box, the athlete will stand in front of the box. The athlete should perform a countermovement jump as was described in the last exercise, but focus on jumping onto the box. The athlete will land on the box with the whole foot, landing on flat feet. Have the athlete step down, reset, and repeat.

Depth Jump

Depth jumps are an advanced exercise that should only be performed by athletes with plyometric experience and consistent landing technique. This exercise begins with the athlete standing on a box. The athlete should step off the box and land in a quarter squat, with the glutes and hamstrings absorbing the impact. Without pausing in the landing, the athlete should explode up and jump as high as possible.

Horizontal Plyometrics

Horizontal plyometrics are important for athletes that want to run fast, jump, or throw. These exercises teach the horizontal application of force, which is a quality that is difficult to develop in the weight room. Horizontal plyometrics are also learned in a progression:
- Standing long jump
- Standing triple jump
- Hurdle hop
- Box jump

Standing Long Jump

This exercise is used extensively in testing and teaches the athlete how to use lower body strength and power. To perform this exercise, have the athlete face the course with the feet hip-width apart. The hands should be at the sides. The athlete should quickly move into a quarter squat. As that squat is being executed, the arms should swing back. Without pausing, the athlete should throw the body forward by jumping and swinging the arms forward.

Standing Triple Jump

This exercise should only be performed by athletes who are proficient at the standing long jump. It is challenging because it requires landing and jumping off one leg at a time. For this exercise, the athlete will face the course with the feet hip-width apart and their hands should be at their sides. The athlete should quickly move into a quarter squat, with their arms being swung back as they move into the squat. Without pausing, the athlete will throw the body forward by jumping and swinging the arms forward. They should land on one foot. Without pausing, they will jump off that foot and land on the other foot. Without pausing, they will jump off that foot and land on both feet.

Hurdle Hop

The hurdle hop drill is done for distance. Set up the hurdles for the desired distance. This drill is like performing the standing long jump, except the athlete must also jump over the hurdle. These hurdles can range from mini-hurdles all the way to track hurdles. To increase the difficulty, the hurdles can cover a greater distance (10 yards instead of five yards, for example), they can be higher, or they can be positioned farther apart.

Box Jump

In the vertical plyometrics section, box jumps were a single effort that was being done to a height. This drill involves a series of boxes that the athlete must jump over. The boxes can be of various heights, set closer together or farther apart, and can be conducted for various distances, depending upon the desired level of difficulty and the athlete's experience/conditioning level.

Throws

Throws, generally with weighted medicine balls, are an important tool for athletes. These exercises teach the athlete how to transfer lower body strength and power to an external object that he is holding. This section will cover the following throws:

- Backward toss
- Forward toss

Backward Toss

This exercise is a good developer of vertical power. It is sometimes used to evaluate this quality with track and field athletes. For this exercise, the athlete will face away from the course and stand with their feet hip-width apart. The medicine ball should be held in front of the body with straight arms. The athlete will quickly move into a quarter squat. As this is done, the medicine ball will quickly be swung down between the legs. Without pausing, the athlete should jump up and throw the medicine ball behind the body, attempting to throw it as far backward as possible.

Forward Toss

This exercise develops horizontal power. For this exercise, the athlete will face the course, standing with the feet hip-width apart. The medicine ball should be held in front of the body with straight arms. The athlete should quickly move into a quarter squat and swing the medicine ball down between the legs. Without pausing, the athlete will jump up and throw the medicine ball as far forward as possible.

Advanced Drills

Up to this point, many movement skills have been treated in isolation. For example, shuffle to the right for five yards. Unfortunately, they are not used that way in athletics. As a result, athletes have to work on how to incorporate multiple skills, multiple stimuli, and their reaction time after they have mastered the fundamentals. This section will not be a comprehensive listing of drills, but it will provide enough to get a coach started. This section will cover the following types of advanced drills:

- Drills that combine two skills
- Drills that combine multiple skills
- Reactive drills

Drills That Combine Two Skills

These drills are meant to be an intermediate step for athletes. The act of combining two skills forces the athlete to process more, perfect their techniques, and begin applying the individual skills to more real-life situations. This is done at first using two skills (start/stop, shuffle/turn, etc.) to help keep these tasks from being overwhelming.

A fast sprint is important for athletes, but non–track and field athletes need to be able to stop unexpectedly and then start back up again. Starting and stopping drills combine these two skills. One of the easiest ways to develop this combination of skills is to set up three cones 5 to 10 yards apart. Use the first cone as the start line. Have the athlete sprint to the second cone. Approaching the second cone, the athlete should chop the steps and lower the center of gravity to come to a complete stop. The athlete then sprints to the third cone (the finish line). After the athlete can execute the movements proficiently, the cones can be removed, and the athlete can perform these movements reacting to the coach's commands.

In many instances, an athlete has to jump up, grab the ball, or deflect a shot, and then land and do something else. Isolated jumps are effective at improving how high or how far an athlete can jump, but they don't resemble how this skill is used in sports. Combining jumping with sprinting is an effective way to teach the athlete to jump and then react to the ground. These drills can be as simple as having the athlete perform a countermovement jump or a standing long jump and then sprinting for a desired distance immediately upon landing. The ball can also be incorporated.

Sprinting and jumping can also be combined with throwing the medicine ball. For example, the athlete can perform a forward toss with the medicine ball and then, immediately upon releasing the ball, sprint for a desired distance. An athlete can perform a medicine ball throw and then a desired jump. These drills help to make the exercises a little more relevant to the athlete's situation on the playing field.

Drills That Combine Multiple Skills

As an athlete progresses in terms of their movement skills, the drills need to become more like the situations they encounter on the playing field. Examples of these drills include the following:
- Shuffle/turn/sprint
- Backpedal/turn/sprint
- Sprint/backpedal/sprint
- Pattern drills

Shuffle/Turn/Sprint

The shuffle is meant to be a transitional move. It is not meant to be something that athletes do for 15 to 20 yards. With that in mind, it's important to teach the athlete how to use this skill to maximum effect. This drill can become sport-specific, so this drill will be covered using two different turning strategies. First, set up three cones. The first cone is the start line, the second cone will be five yards from the start line, and the third cone will be 10 yards from the second cone. The athlete will stand behind the first cone so that the right side faces the course. The athlete should get into the athletic ready position. Next, the athlete will shuffle to the right until reaching the second cone. At the second cone, the athlete will pivot on the left foot while stepping out with the right (Figure 9-11). The athlete should sprint through the third cone.

Figure 9-11. Turning from the shuffle

Some sports, like baseball, use a crossover step to turn. In this case, the athlete will shuffle to the second cone. Upon reaching the second cone, the athlete will pivot so that the feet are at 45-degree angles (Figure 9-12). The athlete should step across with the left foot, and then sprint through the third cone (Figure 9-13).

Figure 9-12. Pivot, preparing for the crossover step

Figure 9-13. Crossover step

Backpedal/Turn/Sprint

The backpedal is another transitional skill. Like shuffling, it's too slow to be performed for 15 to 20 yards effectively in sporting situations. As a result, athletes need to understand how to use it and then go into different movement patterns. To teach this skill, set up three cones just like in the shuffling drill described previously. Begin the drill with the athlete facing away from the course, standing next to the first cone. The athlete will backpedal to the second cone. At the second cone, the athlete should pivot toward the right, using the left foot as the pivot foot. The athlete should step around with the right foot until he has turned 180 degrees and is now facing the third cone. The athlete should sprint through the third cone.

Sprint/Backpedal/Sprint

Sometimes, athletes need to move both forward and backward. A good way to teach this movement is to set five or six cones up in a line. Have the athlete stand next to the first cone and face the course. The athlete will run to the third cone, stop, and then backpedal to the second cone. Next, the athlete should run to the fourth cone, stop, and then backpedal to the third cone. The athlete should keep running forward two cones and backpedaling one until the course is completed.

Pattern Drills

Pattern drills are useful for teaching athletes to shift movement patterns quickly. Care must be taken, though, to prevent the athlete from learning the drill as opposed to learning agility that can be applied to the sport. An example of a pattern drill can be seen in Figure 9-14. The athlete should begin by standing next to cone 1, facing straight ahead. The athlete should shuffle to cone 2, turn and sprint to cone 3. Next, the athlete will run around cone 3 and run to cone 4, stop, and shuffle to cone 5. From cone 5, the athlete should sprint to cone 6, turn, and sprint to the finish line at cone 7.

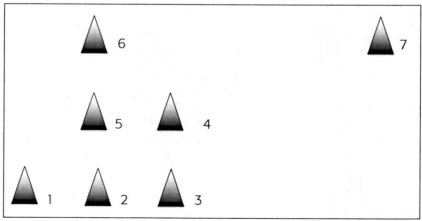

Figure 9-14. Sample pattern drill

Reactive Drills

Reactive drills are the most advanced speed/agility drills and are only for athletes that have consistently solid technique. These drills come the closest to combining speed and agility skills with the unpredictability of the game. These drills can incorporate the ball, the coach, or other players. Examples of reactive drills include the following:

• React to the coach
• Box drill
• Line drill

React to the Coach

The first example of a reactive drill involves the athlete lining up in front of the coach. On command, the athlete sprints toward the coach. The coach will randomly instruct the athlete what to do: run backward, run in a specified direction, stop, shuffle, and so forth. The athlete must react to the coach's instruction and perform the movement correctly.

Box Drill

The second example is shown in Figure 9-15. It involves setting up two 5 x 5 yard boxes. One athlete lines up next to the cone designated by A. The second athlete lines up next to the cone designated by B. Athlete A can move any way he desires provided that he stays within the box. Athlete B must match the movement patterns of Athlete A. The goal is for Athlete A to shake Athlete B, while Athlete B is attempting to stay with Athlete A. Normally, this drill is performed for 15 to 30 seconds. After a rest, the players switch places.

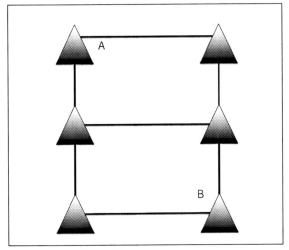

Figure 9-15. Box drill

Line Drill

The final example of a reactive drill is a simple line drill. For this drill, place two cones five yards apart. Draw an imaginary line between the cones. One athlete stands on each side of the line, and they face each other. On command, one athlete attempts to move back and forth, shaking the other athlete. The second athlete tries to keep the first athlete in front of him at all times. Both athletes must remain within the cones. This drill is normally performed for 15 to 30 seconds. After a rest, the players switch roles.

Part III PUTTING EVERYTHING TOGETHER

The final part of this book applies everything that has been covered and puts it together. At some point, exercises must be integrated into a larger program to help improve the athletes' performance in their sport. This part has three chapters: using the tools, long-term training, and applications.

The tools that have been covered in this book all have strengths, weaknesses, and some things for which they are better suited. This is important to understand because money, space, and time are all finite, and a coach wants to make the best use of all of these things when organizing a training program. Chapter 10 describes those strengths and weaknesses, explores for which goals each tool is best, and then makes suggestions for how to use each tool in a larger program.

Having determined how to implement the various tools, it's time to develop the athlete's training program. This process is often made too complicated and frequently has to be changed when the program meets the athlete. Chapter 11 covers how to do so in a manner to move the athlete's development in the direction you want it to go while still remaining flexible.

Finally, the last chapter of the book provides examples of how to bring all this information together. Some of the examples involve short-term goals (for example, increasing an athlete's vertical jump). Others involve how to organize a year's worth of training. These examples are meant to illustrate how to apply all the principles covered as well as how to integrate multiple strength and conditioning tools.

Chapter 10 Using the Tools

So far, this book has covered the following tools that can be used in a strength and conditioning program: free weights, kettlebells, suspension training, heavy ropes, sandbags, and speed/agility/plyometrics. This chapter is going to help the coach and athlete to wade through this information and determine not only which tools are going to be best for their situation, but also to cover how to use each tool as part of a larger strength and conditioning program.

Advantages of Each Tool

Each of the tools that have been covered in this book has advantages. These advantages must be carefully weighed against the disadvantages of each tool and, along with that for which each tool is most effective, must be factored into any decisions to use them. In addition to the various tools having advantages and disadvantages, the different ways that each tool may be employed must be factored in. This aspect will be considered later in this chapter.

Free weights include exercises performed with barbells, dumbbells, and even bodyweight. They have advantages over other pieces of equipment. First, they allow for a great deal of exercise variety. Literally hundreds of exercises can be performed with them that are not restricted by the design of a machine. Second, they are extremely effective tools to develop muscle mass, strength, and power. Third, they require the development and use of stabilizing muscles to balance between the two sides of the body. Finally, they are relatively inexpensive, with a barbell costing a few hundred dollars and weight plates costing a few hundred more.

Kettlebells have several of the advantages of free weights. A great deal of exercise variety is possible. They can be used to increase muscle mass, strength, and power. They can be used as a metabolic conditioning tool. Due to the unilateral nature of kettlebells, they develop balance, coordination, and proprioception. Kettlebells also require a small facility footprint, requiring enough room for the athlete to move.

Suspension training also allows for a wide variety of exercises to be performed. They are great tools for developing the ability to control an athlete's body and can be useful in conditioning workouts. Suspension training requires the development of a great deal of balance and proprioception as well as the development of stabilizing muscles.

Most heavy rope exercises are total body exercises. They are effective tools for developing balance and coordination as well as metabolic conditioning. As with the other tools, a wide variety of exercises can be used with heavy rope exercises.

Many of the exercises performed with free weights can be performed with sandbags. The sand in the sandbag shifts during the exercise, which requires the athlete to develop proprioception, balance, coordination, and stabilizing muscles in a unique manner. In some ways, this approach is more applicable to the unpredictable real world of athletics. Sandbags are also an ideal tool for multi-planar strength training.

Speed, agility, and plyometric exercises are effective at increasing an athlete's ability to accelerate, achieve maximal velocity, and express power. These tools come the closest to applying strength and power to a sport. A wide variety of exercises can be performed, everything from carefully choreographed drills to more random exercises that simulate real life. Most of these exercises can be done with minimal equipment (open space and a few cones).

Disadvantages of Each Tool

It should be recognized by the coach that no training tool is perfect. Each tool described in this book has disadvantages. Some of these disadvantages may be deal-breakers, depending upon a coach's situation and resources.

With free weights, the first disadvantage is that they require space to perform the exercises safely. This mainly applies to barbells because the 45-pound barbells are seven feet long. This means they require an extra two feet in either direction (or 11 feet of space width) for the exercises. This is not counting space in front of the athlete or behind them. While dumbbells don't require that kind of space, a facility needs a lot of them to allow for a variety of weights in order to provide a training effect. A full set of dumbbells for athletes will have to range from very light (five pounds) to very heavy (100 pounds plus), this many dumbbells will take up a great deal of storage space and will cost several thousand dollars to purchase. Some free weight exercises require special equipment, which is more expensive than normal barbells and dumbbells. For example, to perform the Olympic lifts safely, rubber bumper plates and wooden platforms are needed so that the barbells can be safely dropped. Finally, these exercises require a great deal of coaching and spotting to be performed safely and effectively.

Kettlebells are expensive, costing several times what weight plates and dumbbells cost. To use them effectively in a team conditioning situation, many kettlebells of many sizes must be purchased. Not only is this expensive, but it takes up a great deal of space. The weight can be increased using kettlebells (i.e., an athlete can use a heavier kettlebell), but this requires having more sizes of kettlebells on hand. Many of these exercises require a great deal of skill to prevent injuries. While a great number of testimonials speak to the effectiveness of this tool, very little research on kettlebells is available.

Suspension trainers require a great deal of space and, for maximum usefulness, an attachment to a height. To be used in a team environment means that, at a minimum, at least every other athlete will need his own trainer. Suspension trainers can be expensive, especially if considering purchasing enough for a team to use effectively. The ability of suspension training exercises to add muscle mass, strength, and power is extremely limited, though they are good for developing endurance.

Heavy ropes also require a great deal of space to safely perform the exercises. In addition, a number of ropes must be purchased to be used in a team environment. Heavy ropes can be expensive. The ability to overload these exercises is also a challenge for a coach, making these a great tool for metabolic conditioning, but limited for the development of muscle mass, strength, and power.

Sandbags require space to perform the multi-planar exercises that are unique to them. To be used in a team environment, a great number of these bags (along with the sand) must be purchased. These exercises have a skill component which takes time and practice. They are limited in the amount of weight they can hold and this can be imprecise to determine. In addition, there is always the fear/possibility of a spill, especially with regular, intense use.

Speed, agility, and plyometric exercises require open space and the proper surface on which to perform them safely and effectively. They also require a great deal of technique to be effective, safe, and to transfer to the sport for which the training is being performed. Each sport, and sometimes each position in each sport, has movement patterns unique to it and this can make speed, agility, and plyometric training extremely challenging for a coach.

When considering the variety of tools that are available in a strength and conditioning setting today, the challenge lies in the fact that only a limited amount of time is available to train, athletes have a limited capacity to recover from training, the budget to purchase training equipment is limited, and a limited amount of space is available for training. It is hopefully apparent that it isn't practical for most sport conditioning situations to use every possible tool, which means that coaches must make a choice based upon the advantages, disadvantages, and best uses of each of the tools covered in this book. The next part of this chapter will cover the uses for each tool.

Suggested Uses of Each Tool

Free weights should form the foundation of an athletic strength and conditioning program. They should form the bulk of exercises designed to increase muscle mass, increase strength, and teach the application of strength via the Olympic lifts and their variations. In most team situations, this goal is most efficiently achieved by using barbell exercises for the majority of the training with some supplemental dumbbell exercises. Three to four athletes can exercise at each barbell station, spot, provide technical feedback, and help motivate the exercising athlete.

In an athletic team environment, kettlebells will be most useful in a warm-up situation and in a metabolic conditioning situation. Most facilities and programs will not have the resources and space to have a set of kettlebells comprehensive enough for entire teams to get effective muscle mass and strength increasing exercises. In most situations this goal can be accomplished with 20- to 50-pound kettlebells, trying to ensure there is enough for at least every other athlete. This way, one athlete could be exercising with the kettlebell while the other is performing a different exercise.

Suspension trainers have several uses in an athletic strength and conditioning setting. First, it should be realized that they can be set up at each squat rack. This placement would allow them to be easily incorporated into strength and conditioning workouts. They can be used for warm-ups, rehab, core training, or to supplement free weight exercises (for example, perform a fly with the suspension trainer after a free weight bench press).

Heavy ropes can also be set up at each squat rack. These exercises will be most effective as warm-ups, core training, or for metabolic conditioning. Note that while they can be set up at each squat rack, enough room must be available for the exercises to be performed properly.

Sandbags will be useful for helping with balance, proprioception, and multi-directional force application. They are going to be best employed as a supplementary exercise to free weights. For example, an athlete may perform power cleans, back squats, and Romanian deadlifts with the free weights, and then use the sandbags for a rotational lunge.

Speed, agility, and plyometric exercises are most effectively used in their own workouts. When they are combined with other exercise modes (for example, put at the end of a strength training workout), they are not as effective as they would be if used on their own. Plyometrics are occasionally combined with slow, heavy strength training exercises (this combination is called a complex) to maximize training time and to serve as a cue for the athlete's nervous system (the heavy strength training exercise recruits a large number of motor units, following it with a power move helps to take advantage of that recruitment).

Program Design Thoughts

Unless strength and conditioning is being broken up into multiple sessions, in the ideal world, strength and conditioning exercises should have an order. First, the athlete should warm up. Second, exercises requiring speed, power, or a great deal of technique should be performed. Third are the slower, multi-joint exercises. Next are any isolation exercises. Finally, metabolic conditioning should be undertaken. If time allows, then different training sessions can be devoted to different tools. Figures 10-1 and 10-2 show different examples of how this could be accomplished. Figure 10-1 illustrates how to incorporate these aspects into each training session during a week. Figure 10-2 illustrates how to spread the various tools out over the course of a week.

Monday	Wednesday	Friday
Warm-up, 10–15 minutes	Warm-up, 10–15 minutes	Warm-up, 10–15 minutes
5x10-meter sprints	Agility drills, 10–15 minutes	5x60-meter sprints
5x10-meter bounds	Medicine ball throws, 10x	Stride length drills, 3x
Power clean—hang—above the knee, 3x6x60%	Push jerk, 3x6x60%	Power snatch—hang—above the knee, 3x4x60%
Back squats, 3x8–12x70%	Bench press, 3x8–12x70%	Front squats, 3x6–10x60%
Romanian deadlifts, 3x8–12	Dumbbell bench press, 3x12–15	Good mornings, 3x12–15
Kettlebell circuit, 10 minutes consisting of 30 seconds on and 15 seconds off	Pull-ups, 3xMax	Incline press, 3x12–15
	Biceps/triceps, 3x12–15	Bent-over rows, 3x12–15
	Suspension training circuit, 10 minutes consisting of 30 seconds on and 15 seconds off	Military press, 3x12–15
		Heavy rope circuit, 10 minutes consisting of 30 seconds on and 15 seconds off

Figure 10-1. Sample workouts illustrating how to incorporate each training tool into a session

The workouts in Figure 10-1 bring everything together in each training session. The athlete performs sprints, plyos, Olympic lifts, strength training, and then ends with conditioning. As written, these workouts would take about an hour each. This type of training session would be ideal for a high school athlete or even a college freshman. The challenge is that the number of exercises, the intensity, and the volume that is possible in these workouts are very limited due to the fact that the athlete will not be able to sustain their intensity. In addition, there may be challenges with mental focus caused by switching from different types of training (a fast sprint requires a different focus than a long kettlebell circuit). Figure 10-2 presents an alternative, where the workouts are broken up into several training sessions.

The workouts in Figure 10-2 represent something that would be performed by a collegiate or elite athlete. Essentially, the workouts train two things each day, with the exception of Wednesday, which is meant to be an active recovery day. Monday trains whole-body maximal strength and short distance speed/agility. Tuesday trains power, both in the weight room and via plyometrics. Wednesday is a conditioning workout. Thursday develops power. Friday consists of higher volume strength training combined with higher volume speed/agility training. The idea is to match up the various workouts so that they have similar mental/physical demands on the athlete.

Once the tools have been selected and the structure of the workouts has been determined, the variables associated with the exercises can be programed. These variables include the volume (the amount of work done), the intensity (the difficulty of the work done), and the amount of rest (between sets and between workouts). Figure 10-3 presents some general guidelines, depending upon mode of exercise and training goal.

	Monday	Tuesday	Wednesday	Thursday	Friday
Strength Training	Back squats, 3x4–8x75–85% Romanian deadlifts, 3x4–8 Bench press, 3x4–8x75–85% Bent-over rows, 3x4–8 Military press, 3x4–8	Power snatch—hang—knee, 3x4x60% Clean pulls, 3x6x70% Push jerk, 3x4x60%		Power clean, 3x4x60% Split jerk, 3x4 Snatch pulls, 3x6x70%	Lunges, 3x12–15 each leg Superset: Back raises, 3x12–15, and incline press, 3x12–15 Superset: Calves, 3x12–15, and one-arm dumbbell rows, 3x12–15 each arm Superset: Front raises, 3x12–15, and side raises, 3x12–15 Superset: Rear deltoid raises, 3x12–15, and dumbbell shrugs, 3x12–15 Superset: Biceps/triceps, 3x12–15
Speed/Agility Training	Sprinting technique drills, 10–15 minutes 3x5-yard sprints, crouching starts 5x20-yard sprints Start/stop agility drills, 3–5x Backpedal agility drills, 3–5x				Sprinting technique drills, 10–15 minutes Stride length drills, 3x40–60 yards 5x40-yard sprints Shuffle agility drills, 3–5x Turning agility drills, 3–5x

Figure 10-2. Sample training sessions that split up training tools across an entire week

	Monday	Tuesday	Wednesday	Thursday	Friday
Conditioning			Circuit (perform each exercise for 30 seconds, rest one minute after circuit, perform circuit three times): Kettlebell swings Rope slams Kettlebell cleans One-handed rope slams Kettlebell snatches Rope woodchoppers Kettlebell jerks Rope circles Kettlebell get-ups Rope circles		
Plyometrics		Medicine ball rear toss, 5x Box jumps, 3x5		Hurdle hops, 3x5 yards Medicine ball front toss, 10x	

Figure 10-2. Sample training sessions that split up training tools across an entire week (cont.)

Goal	Tool	Intensity	Volume	Rest
Hypertrophy	Free weights Kettlebells	70–85% 1 RM	3–5 sets of 6–15 reps/set	30–60 seconds between each set 48 hours between muscle groups
Strength	Free weights Kettlebells	> 80% 1 RM	3–5 sets of 1–6 reps/set	120 seconds between each set 48 hours between sessions
Power	Free weights Plyometrics	60–80% 1 RM 100%	3–5 sets of 1–6 reps/set 5–10 repetitions	120 seconds between each set 48 hours between sessions
Speed	Sprints Resisted sprints Assisted sprints Technique drills Stride length drills Stride frequency drills	100%	Depends upon goal: Acceleration: up to 20 meters, total volume no more than 500 meters Maximal velocity: up to 100 meters, total volume no more than 1,000 meters Speed endurance: up to 300 meters, total volume no more than 1,000 meters	Full recovery between each sprint 48 hours before training each goal
Agility	Technique drills Choreographed drills Reactive/random drills	100%	Depends upon the drill; usually drills are repeated 3–5 times	Full recovery 48 hours between sessions
Conditioning	Kettlebells Heavy ropes Suspension trainers Sandbags	100%	Sport-specific	Sport-specific

Figure 10-3. Program design variables according to goal

Based upon the information covered in this book, Figure 10-3 provides some recommendations for strength and conditioning training variables. Some important things should be noted about the figure. First, plyometrics, speed work, agility training, and conditioning workouts are meant to be done at 100 percent intensity. Note that it is not the same as 100 percent of 1 RM. In speed training, it means sprinting as fast as possible. In agility training, it means running the drill at full speed. For plyometrics, it means jumping as high/far/fast as possible. For conditioning, it means giving everything during each work interval. Second, note that the volume and rest periods for conditioning work is going to be sport-specific, because every sport has different needs. For example, American football will have different conditioning needs than soccer. Even within a sport, different positions may have different needs. In American football, the kicker and the right tackle will have different conditioning needs due to the differences in what their positions do.

Chapter 11 is going to take this information, as well as the information from previous chapters, and apply it to long-term program design. The final chapter of this book will provide examples of how to incorporate all of this information into achieving specific goals for an athlete.

Chapter 11 Long-Term Training

A large number of tools can potentially be used in a strength and conditioning program. Understanding the tools and their uses is important, but they will not be helpful if they are not incorporated into a program that is designed to enhance an athlete's performance. This chapter will cover how to put together a long-term program designed to enhance performance.

Determine the Peaks

The first step in planning a strength and conditioning journey is to determine the goal the athlete is trying to achieve. This may be to perform at his best during a competitive season, or it may be to be at his best at a specific moment in time (like the world championships). Normally, the time around this peak is considered to be the competition period of training. If it is based around a specific event, then it normally lasts four weeks and ends with that event. If it is based around a competitive season, then it usually makes up the entire season.

Assess the Athlete

The second step is to determine where the athlete is currently. This assessment will help to drive the athlete's training as he attempts to be at his best when it is important. The assessment should be influenced by the following:

- The needs of the sport
- The athlete's history

The Needs of the Sport

Each sport—and in some cases, each position within the sport—has unique strength and conditioning needs. The sport's movement patterns, work:rest ratios, and injury patterns should all be factored into selecting tests. For example, a 10,000-meter runner is going to need a different battery of tests then a goalkeeper in soccer.

The Athlete's History

An athlete's age, training age, familiarity with exercises, and injury history will influence the assessment process. Younger athletes may have a more generic assessment process as there isn't a need for event-specificity with them yet. Athletes that do not have a great deal of training history may not have consistent enough technique on some exercises to evaluate their strength. For example, if an athlete has poor technique on the power snatch, then a 1 RM test probably isn't appropriate. Lastly, the injury history is going to influence the assessment process. For example, an athlete with a history of hamstring injuries is going to need to have quadriceps and hamstring strength evaluated to help prevent future reoccurrences.

The needs of the sport, combined with the athlete's history, frame the assessment process for an athlete. Once a coach understands those things, the coach is able to select a battery of tests to help determine how prepared the athlete is for performance, how well the athlete is progressing as a result of training, and whether the training program is effectively meeting the needs of the athlete and the sport.

Develop the Structure

Through understanding when the athlete needs to peak as well as where he is currently based upon testing, it's time to begin the process of organizing the training. This step involves dividing the training up into structural units. While this process is somewhat arbitrary, it helps because it makes a huge task smaller and more manageable. Long-term planning is divided into several units:

- *Macrocycles:* Macrocycles can either be viewed as an entire training year or as the time between the last peak and the next peak.
- *Periods:* The three types of periods in a macrocycle are the preparatory period (the time during which the athlete is getting into shape), the competition period (the time that the athlete is peaking), and the recovery period (the time between the last competition and the start of the next preparatory period).
- *Phases:* Phases are divisions of periods. The preparatory period is divided into a general preparation phase (foundational fitness) and a special preparation phase (fitness developed in the general preparation phase is applied to the event). The competition period is divided into a pre-competition phase (a sharp increase in intensity as the athlete begins the peaking process) and the competition phase (the athlete peaks and maintains that peak).
- *Mesocycles:* Mesocycles are divisions of a phase and typically last two to six weeks (four weeks is the norm). Dividing each phase into mesocycles makes the planning process more manageable.
- *Microcycles:* Generally, microcycles are divisions of the mesocycle and normally last one week.

Figure 11-1 shows an example of breaking a training year (i.e., a macrocycle) down into periods, phases, and mesocycles. From the figure, the preparatory period makes up the bulk of the year, with the general preparation phase consisting of four mesocycles

Macrocycle	2014											
Period	Preparatory Period						Competition Period					Recovery Period
Phase	General Preparation Phase				Special Preparation Phase		Pre-Competition Phase	Competition Phase				Recovery Phase
Mesocycle	I	II	III	IV	V	VI	VII	VIII	IX	X	XI	XII

Figure 11-1. Sample breakdown of a training year into periods, phases, and mesocycles

and the special preparatory phase consisting of two mesocycles. The competition period is the next largest part of the year with the pre-competition phase consisting of one mesocycle and the competition phase consisting of four mesocycles. The recovery period completes the year and consists of one mesocycle.

The lengths of periods and phases have no hard and fast rules. Normally, the competition period lasts the entire competitive season or lasts four weeks around the major competition. It is normally preceded by a four-week pre-competition phase. For example, for an American football player, the competition period would last from September through December or January, with a four-week pre-competition phase (i.e., training camp) in August. For an Olympic weightlifter, on the other hand, the competition period would consist of the four weeks around the world championships. It's normal for the recovery period to last for two to four weeks. The rest of the year is the preparatory period, with about two thirds of the preparatory period consisting of the general preparation phase.

Some athletes have more than one competition period. For example, collegiate track and field has an indoor season and an outdoor season. Olympic weightlifters may compete in more than one meet. In these cases, there may be several competition periods. Figure 11-2 provides a sample annual breakdown for a collegiate track and field athlete.

Macrocycle	2014											
Period	Preparatory Period I					Competition Period I (Indoors)		Preparatory Period II	Competition Period II (Outdoors)			Recovery Period
Phase	General Preparation Phase		Special Preparation Phase		Pre-Competition Phase	Competition Phase		Special Preparation Phase	Competition Phase			Recovery Phase
Mesocycle	I	II	III	IV	V	VI	VII	VIII	IX	X	XI	XII
Month	Aug	Sep	Oct	Nov	Dec	Jan	Feb	Mar	Apr	May	Jun	Jul

Figure 11-2. Sample organization for a two-peak athlete

For the collegiate track and field athlete, the year begins in August (mesocycle I) and includes two competitive periods (indoors and outdoors). This athlete has competitive periods separated by another preparatory period to take some time to address any deficiencies that were revealed during the first competitive period.

Determine the Broad Goals and Tools for Each Period of Training

Once the structure of the training year has been determined—and before getting into exhaustive detail on training programs—the big picture should be developed. Determining the broad goals for each period of training and determining what range of tools will be used will go a long ways toward making the planning process easier for the coach. For most athletes, each period of training shares common goals. However, this is going to be heavily influenced by the athlete's level. For example, mature elite athletes are not going to spend much time or energy on increasing their muscle mass.

Figures 11-3 and 11-4 are examples of determining broad goals and tools for athletes. These figures build on the situations described in Figures 11-1 and 11-2. Figure 11-3 illustrates this for the one-peak athlete described in Figure 11-1. Figure 11-4 describes this for the two-peak athlete described in Figure 11-2.

For a one-peak athlete, Figure 11-3 shows what the focus will be for each period of training as well as the type of tools that will be used to achieve this. The preparatory period is primarily focused on muscle mass, strength, power, and conditioning, with the bulk of the work being done in the weight room or with implements like kettlebells. The competition period is focused on maintaining the work from the preparatory period while enhancing power, speed, and agility. Plyometrics and a wide variety of speed/agility tools are being employed to develop these qualities. The recovery period seeks to get the athlete in shape while giving him a chance to recover from the rigors of the year that just ended. The athlete is encouraged to participate in a variety of recreational sports and use implements like kettlebells and suspension training to maintain or improve conditioning.

Figure 11-4 shows the broad goals by period as well as the tools that will be emphasized for a two-peak athlete, in this case a sprinter. Due to the nature of the athlete's event, a greater focus is placed on the aspects of sprinting (acceleration, maximal velocity, and speed endurance) and on the different tools for speed training. In addition, plyometrics are used earlier in the athlete's training than for the athlete described in Figure 11-3.

Period	Goals	Tools to Achieve
Preparatory	Increase muscle mass	Free weights
	Increase strength	Free weights Sandbags Kettlebells
	Increase power	Free weights (Olympic lifts)
	Improve metabolic conditioning	Kettlebells Heavy ropes
	Some speed/agility development	Technique drills Stride length drills Short sprints
Competition	Increase speed	Technique drills Stride length drills Sprints Resisted sprints
	Increase agility	Technique drills Cone drills Reactive drills
	Increase power	Free weights (Olympic lifts) Plyometrics
	Maintain muscle mass/strength	Free weights
	Maintain metabolic conditioning	Kettlebells Heavy ropes
Recovery	Maintain muscle mass/strength	Kettlebells Suspension training Heavy ropes
	Maintain power/speed/agility	Varied sports
	Improve metabolic conditioning	Varied sports Kettlebells Suspension training Heavy ropes

Figure 11-3. Goals and tools for the sample one-peak athlete

Period	Goals	Tools to Achieve
Preparatory I	Maintain/increase muscle mass	Free weights
	Increase strength	Free weights
	Increase power	Free weights Plyometrics
	Improve acceleration	Sprints Bounds Stick drills
	Maintain maximal velocity	Sprints
	Improve speed endurance	Sprints
Competition I	Maintain muscle mass	Free weights
	Maintain/increase strength	Free weights
	Increase power	Free weights Plyometrics
	Improve acceleration	Sprints Bounds Stick drills Resisted starts
	Improve maximal velocity	Sprints Stride length drills Resisted sprints Assisted sprints
	Maintain speed endurance	Sprints
Preparatory II	Maintain muscle mass/strength	Free weights
	Increase power	Free weights Plyometrics
	Improve acceleration	Sprints Bounds Stick drills Resisted starts
	Improve maximal velocity	Sprints Stride length drills Resisted sprints Assisted sprints
	Maintain speed endurance	Sprints

Figure 11-4. Goals and tools for the sample two-peak athlete

Period	Goals	Tools to Achieve
Competition II	Maintain muscle mass/strength	Free weights
	Maintain power	Free weights Plyometrics
	Improve acceleration	Sprints Bounds Stick drills Resisted starts
	Improve maximal velocity	Sprints Stride length drills Resisted sprints Assisted sprints
	Maintain speed endurance	Sprints
Recovery	Maintain muscle mass/ strength/power	Suspension training Heavy ropes Sports
	Maintain acceleration/maximal velocity/speed endurance	Sports

Figure 11-4. Goals and tools for the sample two-peak athlete (cont.)

Once the broad goals have been developed and a decision has been made about the tools to use, broad decisions can be made about training frequency for each mode of training as well as trends for the volume and intensity. Note that, in this part of the training process, this information does not have to be incredibly detailed.

Figure 11-5 shows a sample of how to broadly plan out the training variables by period and phase for an athlete without going into exhaustive detail too early in the training process. The sample shown is for the one-peak athlete. This plan serves as a skeleton that the coach can flesh out as the training year progresses. Once this has been done, the first four weeks of training can be planned out in great detail.

Plan the Details Four Weeks at a Time

Once the big picture has been developed, it is appropriate to plan the first four weeks of training in detail. Detailed planning that goes beyond this stage is often unsuccessful because too many variables can interfere with the plan. Ideally, the first four weeks of training is planned in detail. After the athlete has completed the first half of that training, the next four weeks can be planned out in detail.

Period	Phase	Mode of Training	Frequency/Week	Volume	Intensity
Preparatory	General	Free weights (hypertrophy)	2	Moderate	Moderate
		Free weights (strength)	1	Low	High
		Free weights (power)	1	Low	Moderate
		Sandbags	1	Moderate	Moderate
		Kettlebells (strength)	1	Moderate	Moderate
		Metabolic conditioning	2	High	Low
		Speed training	1	Low	High
		Agility training	1	Low	High
	Specific	Free weights (hypertrophy)	2	Moderate	Moderate
		Free weights (strength)	2	Low	High
		Free weights (power)	1	Low	Moderate
		Sandbags	1	Moderate	Moderate
		Kettlebells (strength)	1	Moderate	Moderate
		Metabolic conditioning	1	High	Low
		Speed training	1	Low	High
		Agility training	1	Low	High
Competition	Pre-Competition	Speed training	1	Low	High
		Agility training	2	Low	High
		Free weights (hypertrophy)	1	Moderate	Moderate
		Free weights (strength)	2	Low	High
		Free weights (power)	2	Low	Moderate
		Plyometrics	1	Low	High
		Metabolic conditioning	1	Moderate	Low
	Competition	Speed training	1	Low	High
		Agility training	2	Moderate	High
		Free weights (hypertrophy)	0	N/A	N/A
		Free weights (strength)	1–2	Low	Moderate
		Free weights (power)	1–2	Low	Moderate
		Plyometrics	1–2	Low	High
		Metabolic conditioning	0	Moderate	Moderate

Figure 11-5. Broad training variables by period and phase for the one-peak athlete

When planning the first four weeks of training, first plan out the volume and intensity trends. In many programs, a 3+1 step approach is used for volume and intensity. This means that the intensity increases each week for the first three weeks (this also means that the volume decreases over each week for the first three weeks), while the fourth week is an unloading week (reduced intensity, greater volume).

As an example, the first four weeks of the general preparation phase from Figure 11-5 will be used. Recall that the focus is on hypertrophy and conditioning with some strength, power, speed, and agility work thrown in. Figure 11-6 shows how volume and intensity will be distributed over the first four weeks of the general preparation phase. Over the first four weeks, there is a gradual increase in intensity, volume, and sometimes both with an unloading week in week four.

	Week 1	Week 2	Week 3	Week 4
Hypertrophy	M/L	M/M	H/M	H/L
Strength	L/M	L/M	L/H	L/L
Power	L/L	L/M	L/M	L/L
Kettlebells	L/L	L/M	L/M	L/L
Speed	L/H	L/H	L/H	L/H
Sandbags	L/L	L/L	L/L	L/L
Agility	L/H	L/H	L/H	L/H
Conditioning	M/L	M/L	M/M	L/L

Key:

L = Low   M = Medium   H = High

The first letter in each column refers to volume; the second refers to intensity. For example: L/H refers to low volume, high intensity.

Figure 11-6. Volume and intensity distribution for the first four weeks of the general preparation phase of training

Once the volume and intensity has been determined, writing the workouts is fairly easy. Figure 11-7 shows a week's worth of workouts based upon the information from Figures 11-5 and 11-6. As this represents the first week of the general preparation phase, the focus is on getting the athlete into shape. Mondays and Fridays are devoted to total body hypertrophy training and conditioning. Wednesday is devoted to strength/power training as well as limited speed and agility work. Tuesday and Thursday are unscheduled to give the athlete time to recover.

Following this approach, the next four weeks would be planned out as the athlete is advancing through the current mesocycle. This process would then repeat as the year progresses, with the plans being updated as needed. This approach creates a very flexible, relevant strength and conditioning plan.

Focus	Monday	Tuesday	Wednesday	Thursday	Friday
	Hypertrophy Conditioning	Recovery	Strength/Power Speed Agility	Recovery	Hypertrophy Conditioning
Free Weights	Split squats, 3x12–15 each leg Leg press, 3x12–15 Good mornings, 3x12–15 Back raises, 3x12–15 Dumbbell bench press, 3x12–15 Pull-ups, 3xMax Dumbbell shoulder press, 3x12–15 Biceps/triceps, 3x12–15	N/A	Power clean, hang, above the knee, 3x6x60% Push jerks, 3x6x60% Back squats, 3x6–10x80% Romanian deadlifts, 3x6–10 Bench press, 3x6–10x80% Bent-over rows, 3x6–10 Military press, 3x6–10	N/A	Front squats, 3x8–12x60% Lunges, 3x12–15 each leg Reverse hyperextensions, 3x12–15 Calves, 3x12–15 Incline press, 3x12–15 One-arm dumbbell rows, 3x12–15 each arm 3-in-1 shoulders, 3x12–15 each way Biceps/triceps, 3x12–15
Kettlebells	N/A	N/A	Overhead squats, 3x5 each arm Get-ups, 3x5 each side Windmills, 3x5 each side	N/A	N/A
Sandbags	Sandbag cleans, 3x12–15 Lunges with twist, 3x12–15 each leg	N/A	N/A	N/A	N/A
Speed/Agility	N/A	N/A	Speed/agility technique drills, 15–20 minutes 3–5x10-meter sprints Stride length drills, 3–5x	N/A	N/A
Conditioning	Bodyweight circuit, 10–15 minutes	N/A	N/A	N/A	Heavy ropes/suspension training circuit, 10–15 minutes

Figure 11-7. First week of workouts

Chapter 12 Applications

Each of the tools that are used in a strength and conditioning program has a role in the development of the athlete. As this book has already covered, it is important to organize training in an intentional manner so that the athlete can be successful. This chapter will incorporate everything that has been covered to this point and develop strength and conditioning programs to accomplish different short-term and long-term objectives.

Short-Term Objectives

Short-term objectives address an immediate need that can be improved in a few weeks. This section will set up two examples of programs to address short-term objectives; the first deals with improving the vertical jump, and the second deals with improving the 40-yard dash.

Vertical Jump

The vertical jump is an all-out activity that involves jumping off the ground as high as possible. This test is frequently used in sports to evaluate power; as a result, it is very important to athletes. The vertical jump requires strong legs, an ability to express that strength quickly, technique (both jumping and landing safely), and it requires the use of the arms, as they contribute to a successful jump.

Figure 12-1 details a sample program to enhance an athlete's vertical jump. The core of the program involves strength training and plyometrics. Monday is used as a day to develop the strength that is required for a good vertical jump. This is supported by plyometric exercises that enhance jumping and landing techniques. On Wednesday, the focus is on developing explosive power, which is supported by plyometric exercises that enhance vertical power. Friday includes a power exercise (the power snatch) as well as some hypertrophy work on the lower body, which is supported by practicing the vertical jump as well as jumping onto boxes. Tuesday and Thursday are upper body days with some mixture of kettlebells and sandbag training. In this program, heavy ropes, suspension training, and speed/agility training are not being used because this program is focused exclusively on developing the vertical jump. If there had been a need to perform speed/agility exercises, these would have been incorporated into the Monday and Wednesday workouts.

	Monday	Tuesday	Wednesday	Thursday	Friday
Strength Training	Back squats, 5x4–8x80–90% Partial deadlifts, 3x4–8 Good mornings, 3x6–10 Reverse hyperextensions, 3x6–10 Calves, 3x12–15	Bench press, 3x8–12x70–80% Dumbbell incline press, 3x12–15 Pull-ups, 3x12–15 Standing military press, 3x12–15 Biceps/triceps, 3x12–15	Power clean, 3x3x60–70% Front squats + split jerk, 3x4+3x60–70% Clean pulls, 3x6x70–80%	Dumbbell bench press, 3x12–15 Bent-over rows, 3x8–12 One-arm dumbbell rows, 3x8–12 each 3-in-1 shoulders 3x (10 front raises, 10 side raises, 10 rear deltoid raises)	Power snatch, 3x3x60–70% Split squats, 3x8–12 each leg Lunges, 3x8–12 each leg Romanian deadlifts, 3x8–12 Calves, 3x15–20
Plyometrics	Squat jump, stick landing, 10x Ankle hops, 3x10 yards	N/A	Jump and tuck, 10x Medicine ball behind-back toss, 10x	N/A	Vertical jump, 10x Box jump (onto box), 10x
Kettlebells	N/A	Windmills, 3x10 each side	N/A	Get-ups, 3x10 each side	N/A
Sandbags	N/A	Bent-over rows, 3x12–15	N/A	N/A	Lunges with twist, 3x12–15 each side
Heavy Ropes	N/A	N/A	N/A	N/A	N/A
Suspension Training	N/A	N/A	N/A	N/A	N/A
Speed/ Agility	N/A	N/A	N/A	N/A	N/A

Figure 12-1. Sample program—vertical jump emphasis

40-Yard Dash

The 40-yard dash is another all-out activity that involves sprinting a finite distance as quickly as possible. Unlike the vertical jump, a great many technical components to the 40-yard dash can potentially impact performance. These factors include having an explosive start, good acceleration mechanics, understanding when to transition to maximal velocity running mechanics, and being able to maintain maximal velocity. In addition to technique, acceleration, speed, and speed endurance, a good 40-yard dash time requires lower body strength to exert force against the ground, power for an explosive start, and both the hamstrings and shins need to be addressed to prevent injuries.

Figure 12-2 details a sample program to improve an athlete's 40-yard dash. Monday is a day designed to increase strength in the weight room with a total body workout. This day also sees a horizontal plyometric session and a workout focused on the athlete's ability to accelerate. Tuesday is a power workout focused on the entire body. On Wednesday, the athlete performs an upper body workout in the weight room and a conditioning workout using kettlebells, sandbags, suspension trainers, and heavy ropes. Thursday is another lower body workout, followed by horizontal plyometrics, and a speed workout focused on increasing maximum velocity. Friday finishes out the week with another upper body workout.

Long-Term Objectives

Normally, training is put together on an annual basis. When such is the case, it is divided into off-season, pre-season, and in-season. Off-season training seeks to develop and apply a fitness base to the sport. In periodization language this is the preparation period of training. The off-season leads to pre-season, where training is ramped up, an increased focus is placed on sport skills, and the fitness that has been developed is applied directly to the event. This is the beginning of the competition period. Next, the athlete competes in their sport. This may last a single event (for example, the world championships) or may last a number of games. Finally, there is time off after the season for the athlete to rest and recover, and then the entire process begins again. The remainder of this chapter is going to provide generic examples of how to set up training, employing the types of exercises covered in this book, using this type of structure.

Off-Season Training

Off-season training is about developing the foundation to allow the athlete to be successful during the season. Depending on the sport and the level of the athlete, it may last two to eight months. Ideally, each four-week period represents a mesocycle. Most of the off-season would be spent in general preparation training, with the last third being specific preparation training. This example uses three mesocycles to cover the off-season. The first is an introduction to training. The second steps up the intensity and builds upon the skills developed in the first. The last mesocycle sees greater intensity, variety, and complexity than the first two and serves as a transition to the pre-season.

	Monday	Tuesday	Wednesday	Thursday	Friday
Strength Training	Back squats, 5x4–8x80–90% Partial deadlifts, 3x4–8 Good mornings, 3x6–10 Reverse hyperextensions, 3x6–10 Calves, 3x12–15	Power clean, 3x3x60–70% Split jerk, 3x3x60–70% Clean pulls, 3x6x70–80%	Bench press, 3x8–12x70–80% Dumbbell incline press, 3x12–15 Pull-ups, 3x12–15 Standing military press, 3x12–15 Biceps/triceps, 3x12–15	Power snatch, 3x3x60–70% Split squats, 3x8–12 each leg Lunges, 3x8–12 each leg Romanian deadlifts, 3x8–12 Calves, 3x15–20	Dumbbell bench press, 3x12–15 Bent-over rows, 3x8–12 One-arm dumbbell rows, 3x8–12 each 3-in-1 shoulders 3x (10 front raises, 10 side raises, 10 rear deltoid raises)
Plyometrics	Standing long jump, 10x Ankle hops, 3x10 yards	N/A	N/A	Jump over box, 3x10 Medicine ball toss—forward, 10x	N/A
Kettlebells	N/A	N/A	Conditioning circuit	N/A	N/A
Sandbags	N/A	N/A	Conditioning circuit	N/A	N/A
Heavy Ropes	N/A	N/A	Conditioning circuit	N/A	N/A
Suspension Training	N/A	N/A	Conditioning circuit	N/A	N/A
Speed/Agility	Speed technique drills, 10–15 minutes Stick drills, 3x5 yards Crouching starts, 3x5 yards Resisted starts, 3x5 yards Sprints, 5x10 yards	N/A	N/A	Speed technique drills, 10–15 minutes Stride length drills, 3x20 yards run-up + 20-yard sprint Sprints, 5x40 yards Bounds, 3x20 yards	N/A

Figure 12-2. Sample program—40-yard dash emphasis

Figure 12-3 shows the training being done in the first mesocycle. Training is only performed on Monday, Wednesday, and Friday. Keep in mind that this is the "get in shape" phase of training. For strength training, Monday is focused around total body strength. It consists of fundamental multi-joint strength training exercises, and this is the heaviest training of the week. Wednesday is intended to be focused around power, though front squats and good mornings are included at the end of the strength training workout. The Olympic lifts begin to be taught in this phase. Friday is a total body hypertrophy workout, consisting of supersets between upper body work and lower body work. Fundamental plyometrics (mainly focused on proper landing) are introduced on Monday and Wednesday. A conditioning circuit consisting of kettlebells and heavy ropes is performed on Friday. Elementary speed training, mostly focused around technique, is performed on Mondays and Wednesdays. This training is organized around the idea that Monday will be focused on acceleration and Wednesday will be focused on maximal speed training.

Figure 12-4 shows the second mesocycle of training in the off-season, and it is a little more intense than the first mesocycle. The strength training is organized the same with many of the same exercises. Monday is still the heavy day, though the training intensity is higher than in the previous mesocycle. On Wednesday, the Olympic lifting variations have changed as the athlete is becoming more consistent with his technique. Friday is still a total body hypertrophy session. The plyometrics are increasing in their variety as the athlete develops fitness and technique.

Figure 12-5 shows the third mesocycle, the one before the pre-season begins. The strength training is organized in a similar manner as the previous two mesocycles. Monday, being the heaviest day, has the greatest intensity. Wednesday introduces more complex variations of the power clean. Friday introduces a variation of the power snatch and reduces the number of exercises to be performed as part of strength training. The plyometrics are maintained. The speed and agility is expanded, with a dedicated agility session on Friday. Conditioning has been moved to Tuesdays and Thursdays to allow for more time to focus on strength, speed, power, and agility on Monday, Wednesday, and Friday.

Pre-Season Training

Pre-season training is still organized around three strength training sessions per week. However, the sessions are becoming heavier and the exercises are becoming more complex. Figure 12-6 provides a sample week of pre-season training. Friday is now focused around the power snatch exercise, though it still includes summer lower body and upper body work. The plyometrics have been expanded to include box jumps, and a third plyometric day has been added (Friday) to include medicine ball throws. Conditioning remains on Tuesday and Thursday. The speed and agility training has been expanded to increase distances and to add new drills as the athlete's technique improves.

	Monday	Tuesday	Wednesday	Thursday	Friday
Strength Training	Back squats, 3x8–12x70–80% Romanian deadlifts, 3x8–12 Bench press, 3x8–12x70–80% Bent-over rows, 3x8–12 Standing military press, 3x8–12	N/A	Power clean–hang–above the knee, 3x6x60% Clean pulls–hang–knee, 3x6x60% Push jerk, 3x6x60% Front squats, 3x4–8x60–70% Good mornings, 3x8–12	N/A	SS: Lunges and dumbbell bench press, 3x12–15 SS: Split squats and dips, 3x12–15 SS: Back raises and pull-ups, 3x12–15 SS: Reverse hyperextensions and one-arm dumbbell rows, 3x12–15
Plyometrics	Squat jumps, 10x	N/A	Squat jumps, 10x	N/A	N/A
Kettlebells	Two-handed swings, 3x10	N/A	Two-handed swings, 3x10	N/A	Conditioning circuit
Sandbags	N/A	N/A	N/A	N/A	N/A
Heavy Ropes	N/A	N/A	N/A	N/A	Conditioning circuit
Suspension Training	N/A	N/A	N/A	N/A	N/A
Speed/Agility	Speed technique drills, 10–15 minutes 5x10-yard sprints	N/A	Speed technique drills, 10–15 minutes 5x20-yard sprints	N/A	N/A

Key:
SS = Superset (i.e., two exercises whose sets are alternated with little rest between them)

Figure 12-3. Off-season training—first sample mesocycle

	Monday	Tuesday	Wednesday	Thursday	Friday
Strength Training	Back squats, 3x6–10x75–85% Romanian deadlifts, 3x6–10 Bench press, 3x6–10x75–85% Bent-over rows, 3x6–10 Standing military press, 3x6–10	N/A	Power clean—hang—knee, 3x6x60% Clean pulls—hang—below the knee, 3x6x60% Push jerk, 3x6x60% Front squats, 3x4–8x60–70% Good mornings, 3x8–12	N/A	SS: Lunges and dumbbell bench press, 3x12–15 SS: Split squats and dips, 3x12–15 SS: Back raises and pull-ups, 3x12–15 SS: Reverse hyperextensions and one-arm dumbbell rows, 3x12–15
Plyometrics	Squat jumps, 10x Countermovement jumps, 10x	N/A	Long jumps, 10x Hurdle hops, 10 yards	N/A	N/A
Kettlebells	Two-handed swings, 3x10	N/A	Two-handed swings, 3x10	N/A	Conditioning circuit
Sandbags	N/A	N/A	N/A	N/A	Conditioning circuit
Heavy Ropes	N/A	N/A	N/A	N/A	Conditioning circuit
Suspension Training	N/A	N/A	N/A	N/A	N/A
Speed/Agility	Speed technique drills, 10–15 minutes Stick drills, 3x5 yards 5x10-yard sprints	N/A	Speed technique drills, 10–15 minutes 5x20-yard sprints	N/A	N/A

Key:
SS = Superset (i.e., two exercises whose sets are alternated with little rest between them)

Figure 12-4. Off-season training—second sample mesocycle

	Monday	Tuesday	Wednesday	Thursday	Friday
Strength Training	Back squats, 3x4–8x80–90% Romanian deadlifts, 3x4–8 Bench press, 3x4–8x80–90% Bent-over rows, 3x4–8 Standing military press, 3x4–8	N/A	Power clean—hang—below the knee, 3x6x60% Clean pulls, 3x6x60% Push jerk, 3x6x60% Front squats, 3x4–8x60–70% Good mornings, 3x8–12	N/A	Power snatch—hang—above the knee, 3x6x60% Split squats, 3x8–12 each leg Reverse hyperextensions, 3x8–12 Dumbbell bench press, 3x8–12 Pull-ups, 3x8–12 Biceps/triceps, 3x8–12 each
Plyometrics	Squat jumps, 10x Countermovement jumps, 10x	N/A	Long jumps, 10x Hurdle hops, 10 yards	N/A	N/A
Kettlebells	N/A	Conditioning circuit	N/A	Conditioning circuit	N/A
Sandbags	N/A	Conditioning circuit	N/A	Conditioning circuit	N/A
Heavy Ropes	N/A	Conditioning circuit	N/A	Conditioning circuit	N/A
Suspension Training	N/A	N/A	N/A	N/A	N/A
Speed/ Agility	Speed technique drills, 10–15 minutes Stick drills, 3x5 yards 5x10-yard sprints	N/A	Speed technique drills, 10–15 minutes 5x20-yard sprints	N/A	Agility technique drills, 10–15 minutes Pattern drills, 10–15 minutes

Figure 12-5. Off-season training—third sample mesocycle

	Monday	Tuesday	Wednesday	Thursday	Friday
Strength Training	Back squats, 3x1–4x85–95% Romanian deadlifts, 3x1–4 Bench press, 3x1–4x85–95% Bent-over rows, 3x1–4 Standing military press, 3x1–4	N/A	Power clean, 3x3x70% Clean pulls, 3x6x80% Push jerk, 3x3x70% Front squats, 3x4–8x70–80% Good mornings, 3x8–12	N/A	Power snatch—hang—knee, 3x6x60% Snatch pulls—hang—below the knee, 3x6x60% Split squats, 3x8–12 each leg Reverse hyperextensions, 3x8–12 Dumbbell bench press, 3x8–12 Pull-ups, 3x8–12
Plyometrics	Squat jumps, 5x Countermovement jumps, 10x Box jumps, 5x	N/A	Long jumps, 5x Hurdle hops, 10 yards Box jumps, 5x	N/A	Medicine ball toss—behind, 5x Medicine ball toss—front, 5x
Kettlebells	N/A	Conditioning circuit	N/A	Conditioning circuit	N/A
Sandbags	N/A	Conditioning circuit	N/A	Conditioning circuit	N/A
Heavy Ropes	N/A	Conditioning circuit	N/A	Conditioning circuit	N/A
Suspension Training	N/A	N/A	N/A	N/A	N/A
Speed/ Agility	Speed technique drills, 10–15 minutes Stick drills, 3x5 yards Resisted sprints, 3x5 yards 5x10-yard sprints	N/A	Speed technique drills, 10–15 minutes Stride length drills, 3x20 yards 5x40-yard sprints	N/A	Agility technique drills, 10–15 minutes Pattern drills, 10–15 minutes

Figure 12-6. Pre-season training—sample mesocycle

In-Season Training

In-season training means doing enough to maintain fitness, perhaps increase it somewhat, but also save time and energy for expanded sports practices, travel, and competition. Figure 12-7 shows a sample of in-season training. In this example, strength training is only being performed on Monday and Thursday and has been combined with plyometrics. Exercises are performed as complexes. For example, the athlete would perform three power cleans, stand up with the bar, and then perform four front squats. The idea is to maximize the athlete's time in the weight room. Speed training is also reduced, with the acceleration session being dropped. The idea being that acceleration is being developed during the agility training so that once the athlete reaches the in-season, it can be sacrificed. The result is that, on Monday, the focus is on maximum velocity, and on Thursday the focus is on agility. Conditioning is only being performed on Tuesday, though suspension training has been added to make up for the recued upper body work in the weight room. Note that this session (conditioning) could be performed any day of the week that the strength training is not being performed.

The training that has been illustrated in this chapter is progressive in nature. This means that as the athlete moves through the program, they learn more complicated exercises, the volume increases steadily, and the intensity increases. In addition, a gradual shift in the training moves from general, fitness-focused to more sport-specific power-oriented training.

Athletes have a finite amount of time that they can use for training and a finite ability to recover from that training. As a result, it is very important to use that time wisely and get the most benefit from the least amount of time possible. It is also important to organize training sessions so that they complement each other and complement the athlete's sport practices and competition schedule.

	Monday	Tuesday	Wednesday	Thursday	Friday
Strength Training/ Plyometrics	Power clean + front squats, 3x3+4–8x70–80% Clean pulls + Romanian deadlifts, 3x6+4–8x70–80% Good mornings + standing long jump, 3x4–8 + 5 jumps Bench press + medicine ball chest pass, 3x4–8x70–80% + 5 throws	N/A	N/A	Snatch grip deadlift + power snatch–hang–below the knee, 3x4–8+3x60–70% Back squats + countermovement jumps, 3x4–8x70–80% + 5 jumps Bent-over rows + medicine ball toss–front, 3x4–8 + 5 throws	N/A
Kettlebells	N/A	Conditioning circuit	N/A	N/A	N/A
Sandbags	N/A	Conditioning circuit	N/A	N/A	N/A
Heavy Ropes	N/A	Conditioning circuit	N/A	N/A	N/A
Suspension Training	N/A	Conditioning circuit	N/A	N/A	N/A
Speed/Agility	Speed technique drills, 10–15 minutes 5x60-yard sprints Stride length drills, 3x20 yards	N/A	N/A	Agility technique drills, 10–15 minutes Pattern drills, 10–15 minutes Reactive drills, 10–15 minutes	N/A

Figure 12-7. In-season training—sample mesocycle

About the Author

John Cissik has been involved with all levels of the strength and conditioning industry. Currently, he owns Human Performance Services, LLC, which helps coaches address their strength and conditioning needs. He also works as the Director of Fitness and Recreation at Texas Woman's University.

Cissik has a bachelor's degree in kinesiology from the University of Texas at San Antonio, a master's in kinesiology from Texas A&M University, and a master's of business administration with an accounting emphasis from the University of Texas at Dallas. In addition, he holds certifications from the National Strength and Conditioning Association and the National Academy of Sports Medicine, and has been certified by the former U.S. Weightlifting Federation, as well as U.S.A. Track and Field.

Cissik has written extensively about strength and conditioning. His articles have appeared in popular publications, such as *IRONMAN Magazine* and *Muscle and Fitness,* in professional publications, such as *Strength and Conditioning Journal,* and in numerous track and field coaching publications, such as *STACK, Track Coach, Techniques,* and *Modern Athlete and Coach.* John also travels, consults, and speaks extensively about strength and conditioning.

Cissik spends his free time with his family. He coaches baseball, basketball, Special Olympics sports, and athletic/fitness programs for children with special needs. He is also extensively involved in advocacy work on behalf of children with special needs. He can be found on Twitter @jcissik, on Facebook at https://www.facebook.com/HPServices, or on LinkedIn.